before the basics

by bev bos

photographs by
david burton

creating conversations with children

turn the page press

Published by arrangement with The Burton Gallery.

Edited and designed by Kay Glowes.
Cover design by Bryce Camp.
Composed in Sabon by Dwan Typography, Nevada City, California.

Fifth printing, November 1987

ISBN: 0-931540-01-1
Library of Congress Catalogue Card Number: 82-074059

contents

introduction

Interchange with the child

"Back to the basics" is a popular phrase these days, but I have tried to suggest in the title of this book that it is what we do before we present the basics that will create success or failure for our children as they learn. I am convinced that what we do with children before they begin their formal education is crucial to their full mastery of those areas we popularly call "the basics." I am even more deeply convinced that what we do with children before they begin their formal education will be crucial to the rest of their lives.

I have used the word *conversations* in my title to imply the necessity of genuine interchange with the child as part of the learning environment. *Conversation* implies a kind of interchange that proceeds on the basis of a response from the other party. In creating a conversation with a child, we must pick up our cues from the child. Picking up those cues and acting positively on the basis of those cues is the difference between a conversation and a lecture, a conversation and a performance, a conversation and a monologue.

I have also tried to suggest in the title that process rather than product needs to be the heart of our efforts with children. That process must be child-centered; it must always start with the child and involve interchange with the child—an idea that seems terribly obvious, but that is much lacking in the everyday, practical reality of how we deal with children.

I have attempted here to provide parents and teachers of young children with some extended examples of language, music, and movement activities which provide solid prereading language experiences and which depend for their success on the child's participation rather than on our entertaining the child—and thus behaving like the television set whose overpresence in the lives of young children we all deplore and fear.

While neither the philosophy nor the activities I am offering are necessarily original, I hope that you will find in the chapters that follow some slightly different ways of performing activities as well as some practical definitions of child-centered language learning. I have tried to provide a *sense* of how to develop a child-centered approach to language—an approach that will extend to all learning experiences.

I find that I can check my own program by using the following five tests. They are tests of whether an activity leads children out of themselves and into a new experience. I also use the five tests as a kind of checklist when I am considering new materials or activities of any kind. I believe they are tests that anyone could apply, and I further believe that any activities for young children — whether they involve books, stories, songs, games, or sharing—should meet one or more of these criteria:

(1) Does the activity help children toward self-identification or reinforce their self concept positively?

(2) Does the activity encourage children to change or modify presented materials according to their own options and imaginations?

(3) Does the activity encourage children to create—that is, to make a song, story, or game completely out of their own experience?

(4) Does the activity encourage children to interact positively—that is, to choose to work with other children and/or a parent or teacher toward a larger goal?

Gales of laughter

(5) Does the activity promote gales of laughter or heighten a child's sense of fun? Is it, in other words, irresistible?

Ideally, young children should experience all five of these opportunities many times daily—at home and throughout a school year. If an activity doesn't do one or more of these things, that activity is probably at best a waste of time and at worst likely to be destructive of children's attitudes toward themselves, their classmates, and the learning experience itself.

After a discussion of some basic errors that are all too easy to fall into and some suggestions on how to avoid them, I have ordered the chapters that follow according to the tests themselves. You will find that many of the activities and examples pass more than one of the child-centered tests. At the end of the book, I offer a list of books and records that I have found particularly useful and delightful through my years of teaching.

The object of all these suggestions—in fact, the object of this whole book—is to inspire you to go out and find your own additions to the lists as well as your own variations on my five-question method of deciding whether materials are worth your time—and a child's!

child-centeredness: from the inside out

We all want to do the best for our children—both our own and those under our care. We want to see them grow to full potential as happy and productive human beings, capable of love, capable of work. We want to give them the best possible start.

As adults, we must first remember that we are in charge of the settings in which our children develop and discover: we create and control those settings for better or worse. Sometimes, unfortunately, it is for the worse. Why that should be is not very mysterious. Our very desire to do the best for our children makes us nervous. Although we have all been children, we forget what being a child was like. We begin to see children as objects, forgetting that we need to communicate with them or mistrusting our ability to communicate with them. In so doing, we lead them into mistrusting their own sense of what is good for them.

In our nervousness, we make other mistakes. We forget not only what we should know about the child, but what we have come to know about the learning process. The child and the process are not separable: the child's experience is the learning process. We also make the mistake of thinking that be-

Experience as learning

cause we can control the learning environment, we can control the rate of learning: we are impatient for results—at great expense to children. Finally, in our desire to *teach,* rather than to *share experience,* we become mechanical—and sometimes even rather grim.

This book developed out of my own questions to myself about my preschool program. I tried to analyze what it is I do every day and more particularly why it is I don't do things the way I did when I started out. I think I'm good at spotting basic errors parents and teachers fall into because I have fallen into nearly all of those traps myself. What took me so long to recognize the absence of child-centeredness in my own program? I believe, ironically, that it was my desire to do the very best job I could as a teacher coupled with my misplaced idea of what that was.

Most of us have, I think, a tendency to want to entertain our children and students rather than to involve them. We aren't always operating here out of laziness or ego: it isn't necessarily easier to entertain them. As teachers, we sometimes feel, quite incorrectly, that the harder an activity is for us to prepare and present, the more the child will gain from it. Of course, when we have spent hours preparing something—thinking meanwhile more and more of the elegance of the preparation rather than the children for whom it is intended—the temptation to ignore the fact that the project really may not be doing anything for children is almost more than we can withstand.

I have observed for years, for example, that one of the most beneficial and certainly most popular creative art activities with almost all children under ten is the cut-and-color table, which takes no preparation at all beyond setting out the felt pens, choices of paper, scissors, hole punchers, tape, and sticky dots. Children of all ages will work together in this kind of setting — learning to manipulate, talking, laughing, and, most important, creating — each in an individual way.

It's hard to be upstaged by a pair of scissors and a package of sticky dots. It's even harder, in language activities, for a teacher not to be the star. It takes both experience and determination to avoid this trap. When I first started teaching, I knew I had a lot to tell the children—songs to sing, books to read. Most of the songs were fast-paced and fun, and I read the books all the way through—

without stopping, of course. The experience for the children was not entirely negative, but a voice somewhere kept nagging at me, and when I finally stopped to listen, I realized that I was doing many things that weren't doing very much for the children at all. So I tried to change.

Slowly I started letting the children discuss many pages of the book as I read. I would stop. We would examine a picture, asking questions about what they could see. Often they would see details I hadn't. If I would ask them what they thought would happen next, they could frequently come up with wonderfully creative ideas. As this process continued, I began to see marvelous results.

I started to see the children themselves emerging—attempting *their* language, attempting to communicate with me—and at the same time, I could see that they were discovering that they were capable of complicated and delightful communication.

I have often been asked in my workshops how we can allow time for such interruptions—such a slow pace—when there's so much to do. My answer is that if the interruption doesn't happen, it is very likely that learning isn't happening. We need to translate *interruption* as the child's entering the process. If we genuinely believe that language development is at the heart of the learning process, then we must allow time. Not only allowing for, but planning for interruptions is our whole purpose.

Valuing interruptions

Certainly the parent reading to one or two children can observe the same principle. The object isn't the story itself: it's the child's response to the story—especially a verbalized response—that we should be after most of the time.

If we begin thinking of our efforts with children in terms of *their* involvement rather than our own, our days will become much easier and certainly more satisfying.

Why do children so enjoy activities that they can participate in? Because children are quite capable of sensing when they are growing.

Experience isn't simply the best teacher; it is the only teacher. Jean Piaget said it unequivocally:

> Every time we teach a child something, we keep him from inventing it himself.
> . . . That which we allow him to discover by himself . . . will remain with him.

Most of us would say we believe Piaget, but we don't allow our belief to influence us in what we do with our children each day. Instead, we act as if every day must be approached differently, with a new list of tasks, a new set of tests, a new batch of projects. In fact, parents and teachers probably need to think more in terms of approaching every day in the *same* way, with projects that the child can vary according to need and readiness. Repetition when it is imposed from without and poorly thought-out probably deserves the bad press it is currently getting in education, but repetition remains one of the most important keys to learning in young children. They need to do things many, many times in order to master them and then, more important, to feel comfortable doing them—to enjoy doing them. In order to promote learning, the repeated experience must be both carefully thought out for its learning benefits and then, most of the time, be chosen by the child.

I believe the concept of repetition is especially useful when combined with the first four tests I apply to activities as tests of their child-centeredness. Does this activity help the child's sense of identity? Is the activity open-ended—that is, can the child change this material? Does this activity allow the child to create? Does the activity provide a framework for the child to cooperate with others while retaining a sense of self?

Children are open to learning in different ways on different days. Even the nearly-five-year-old who is in a program for a third year will benefit from repeating an activity that is genuinely child-centered, because the older child will be able to use the activity in a different way than it was used the first time around.

Discovery is the key word from Piaget that we need to keep in mind when dealing with the learning process in young children. Too often, formal activities for young children are set up so that right-wrong answers deprive them of the opportunity to discover all the possibilities.

In an effort to avoid the right-wrong trap, I try to think of myself as *sharing* each story, each song with the children. While the word *teaching* implies that something must be done, and done in one correct way—and even young children are quick to pick up on those rather dreary implications—*sharing* implies that I want the child to know this wonderful story, for example, and that I want us to experience the story together—that the child has as much to offer to the process as I do. I try to think of myself not so much as *teacher,* but *sharer.*

One example of the difference between *teaching* and *sharing* that many of you may recognize from your own experience is the Weatherman or Weatherboard present in many preschool and elementary classrooms in the form of a flannelboard, a paper doll, or a decorated board. Some consist of dials with pictures of clouds, lightning, snow, and sun. Some are flannelboard figures that can be dressed appropriately according to the day's weather.

I made my own weather dial with great enthusiasm and used it my first year, but I soon sensed that it was boring the children. After I struggled with accusing them of ingratitude—you are as familiar with those inner dialogues as I am, I'm sure—"Too much television!" "Children aren't what they used to be!"—I reminded myself firmly of something I really believe: that children have a natural thirst for knowledge and growth, and when they begin to be bored, the problem is not likely in them but more likely in either what we are presenting or how we are presenting it. The children didn't like the weatherboard because they are smarter about the weather than the weatherboard gives them credit for being. Childhood is too brief to be taken up with activities that are only time-serving.

For one thing, weather changes—even in the two-and-a-half hours a child may be in a morning or afternoon session. For another, the weatherboard presumes that there are "right answers." Thus, in a weatherboard structure, the marvelous child who wants to dress the weatherman in a bathing suit and provide him with an umbrella becomes "wrong" instead of a child taking creative initiative. What are we doing with a weather*man* anyway? How does the weatherboard allow for the child who can't resist putting snow on the dial out of a desire to see it?

We now do weather outside, where the children and I can be in touch with what we're talking about. What after all is the point of including weather in the curriculum? We step outside or onto the patio and watch, and we *talk* about the weather.

This year, we had much more rain than usual. Everyone, frankly, was very tired of it. In the middle of sharing one day, I said, "Come on! Let's go out and enjoy the weather!"

It was pouring. We ran on the bicycle trail, lifting our heads up and sticking out our tongues to catch the rain. We laughed; we touched each other's wet arms and faces. We talked about the dark clouds, and then we ran back in.

The joy, the sense of play and friendship as we talked was overwhelming. Months later, children would say, "Do you remember when we ran in the rain?" When we talk about the best things we've done, very often a child will say, "The best day was when we ran in the rain!"

A sense of fun

These kinds of activities often drive adults crazy. Often they'll say, "Oh, but they'll catch cold!" The only thing we all caught that day was a sense of fun.

Putting the child at the center of the learning process, then, is exactly what we need to do as a first step toward conquering our nervousness, but more important, toward doing the best for our children. As we see children excited and engrossed, we will build on their successes.

It might be good to consider a few traps at this point. People sometimes connect child-centeredness with self-centeredness and draw all the wrong conclusions. Child-centeredness does not mean permissiveness. It does not mean that the child should control the lives of surrounding adults.

On a parent-child level, however, child-centeredness might translate as the Golden Rule. It means not hesitating to be gentle and kind. It means being willing to stop your shopping or driving to attend to your child's needs. It means dealing sincerely rather than superficially with the individual child and recognizing that no one child is like another, no matter how many child-development books refer to the statistical "average."

Child-centeredness means that we must be astute observers of children; we must know each child "from the inside out." One key is to focus on what the child is feeling. Only the child can tell us what we need to know. An important byproduct of this careful observation is that conventional testing of development will become less significant than long-range observation as a yardstick of development.

Our first thought should be to avoid putting adult ideas into children's heads. We cannot assume that children see things the way we do. For example, I used to tell my own young children to go clean their rooms. They would go in, look around, and not see that anything at all was out of order or needed cleaning. I learned to go in with them and point out—without ill-feeling—the dirty sock under the covers, the moldy sandwich under the bed.

It is admittedly hard to remember what children really are—as opposed to our adult ideas of what they ought to be. I find it easier to remember the realities of childhood by playing what I have come to call the "Children Were Not Born To" game. The list of adult priorities which are emphasized as if they were life-goals in themselves is probably endless—or so it seems to me. I'll give you my list with some comments; you will certainly be able to supply some of your own endings.

Children were not born to wear name tags. When I visit schools in March and children are still wearing them, I'm frankly appalled. Often people say, "I do it so each child recognizes his or her name." This answer always reminds me of the time one of my sons, then in first grade, dissolved in tears and refused to go to school because he had lost his name tag. "They won't know who I am," he wailed. I was struck by the impact that only a few days of school had had on him. When I reminded him that he could always tell them who he was, he cheered up immediately.

Children were not born to wear name tags

A more valid reason for not using name tags has to do with individual recognition. We need to be recognized and loved for ourselves. Imagine how you'd feel if your spouse or parent or child slapped a name tag on you each morning because it was too difficult or bothersome to remember your name.

I have been involved in summer programs that made it necessary to learn the names of fifteen new students each week; we have made a point of knowing all the children's names by the end of the first hour. It's not a question of memory: like many people I know, I often get up from the table, go to the refrigerator, and stand there not knowing what in the world I came for. It is a question of caring. I remember the frightening feeling of being lost in a crowd; I remember the security of having someone greet me by name. I make a do-or-die effort to remember the name of each child.

Children were not born to sit still. When I visit schools and I don't hear children asking questions, arguing, even interrupting, I suspect that there's little learning going on. Children must be actively involved to learn. A little quiet goes a long way.

Children were not born to sit still

Children were not born to stand in line

Children were not born to stand in line. Since most adults I know don't like to stand in line, we must understand if we think about it how awful standing in line is for young children—all that energy and curiosity simply brought to a halt. Of course, it's not. Standing in line is simply an invitation to pinching, poking, shoving, stepping on toes. In the many years I've taught young children, I've rarely found it necessary to line them up for anything. Time is precious. We can sing songs, tell stories, have conversations during the time wasted lining up.

Children were not born to speak with "inside voices"

Children were not born to speak with "inside voices." They can't all shout all the time, all at once, but when a young child—or even an enthusiastic older child—comes running in shouting, "Mom!" "Dad!" "Teacher!" and is met with "That's an outside voice," or "We don't shout inside," I cringe. That raised voice is discovery—joy—wonder—and we need to listen before we ask for quiet.

Children were not born to walk

Children were not born to walk. They were born to run—barefoot, over rocks, through the water, through the mud. We need to give greater recognition to the energy and joy of children.

Children were not born to wear shoes

Children were not born to wear shoes. In our concern for hygiene and safety, we develop amnesia. Give children a break! Remember how good mud feels between the toes?

Children were not born to wear designer clothes

Children were not born to wear designer clothes. What an injustice to young children to mar their joy in discovering art, mud, building materials, sand, paint, or water by the sinking feeling that they have ruined their clothes. No wonder young children often prefer wearing no clothes at all!

Children were not born to be neat

Children were not born to be neat. This is a question of close observation and tact. All of us want children to learn to put away their belongings, but if I observe children engaged in one activity suddenly discovering something more interesting, I don't interrupt the new activity by insisting upon an immediate cleanup of the old. The child's interest in the new discovery is more important than the cleanup. I make a mental note of who's been playing where, and when it's cleanup time, we all pitch in in a cheerful, cooperative effort. When a child has finished an activity and hasn't shown interest in something new, I might encourage a prompt cleanup. There's certainly more to life than always putting away our belongings!

All these thoughts are adult thoughts; children not only don't do these things naturally, they don't even know what the point of doing them is. What were children born to do? To grow into their full potential.

Just as we should not try to put adult ideas into children's heads, we must always remember how long it takes for children to develop and learn all the things we already know. Sometimes it seems we are determined to teach everything at once.

Nowhere is our impatience for the end product more apparent, and probably more damaging, than it is in our pushing children too early into formal learning experiences—particularly reading. We should know better. A generation of research and observation has produced a solid body of evidence that shows the many complex developmental stages children must go through before they will be physically ready to master and retain the skills that literacy demands.

In addition, children need to have experiences before they can attach words to the experiences. They need to know that language belongs to them and to communicate in hundreds of ways—verbal and nonverbal—before they tackle the formal complicated tasks of reading.

Before reading, children need experiences with wind, dirt, mud, water; experiences with other children, grandparents, running, walking, flowers, books, smells, gardens, balls, soft things, hard things, music, moving, trains — to name just a few. Children need experiences—short, happy experiences—with grocery stores, libraries, bookstores. Children need experiences with wood, building, rolling, swinging, clouds, rain. And they need to talk about them, ask questions, point, make noise—in short, to use language with all of their experiences.

Without a solid base of these prereading language experiences, children will be much more likely to founder later. The current emphasis on early reading—at ages three and four—is producing some terrible consequences for many children. If some children are being pushed before they are ready and thus invited into early failure, other children who may show no immediate problems with early mastery of reading skills are also being damaged, I believe, by being deprived of a sufficient foundation and background in language on which to base later formal reading experience. I don't believe we are damaging this second group less than the first: it is as if we are taking early talent as a signal to stunt growth.

Earliest isn't best. Fastest isn't best. If what we want for our children is a lifetime of excellence—in experience, in ability, in knowledge—we must be responsible enough to wait and thorough enough to look at all sides of their development.

There is yet another way in which our nervous concern for our children leads to less-than-effective learning. Learning is a human activity. It needs to be filled with laughter, sometimes with tears, with infinite, painstaking effort; but it must never be mechanical. Child-rearing and education are a serious business. That doesn't mean they have to be a grim business. Rather the contrary. We need to develop a sense of joy in working with young children exactly in proportion to our sense of how important their learning is to us.

We need to re-establish contact with the child in ourselves to converse profitably with the young children around us. We need, for their sakes, to risk: to risk looking silly, to risk losing perfect discipline, to risk showing emotion. What will we gain? A communication that will make the process of learning come alive.

On the last day of school, I don't let any of my children leave without a special hug and a kiss from me. When they're all grouped around me, waiting their turn, many of them are in tears, and I am too. I think it's important that they know I'll miss them and am touched that they'll miss me and each other. Certainly it's important that they see it's all right to have feelings and to show feelings in a learning environment—that learning is laughter and tears as much as it is books and watercolor paints and songs.

I have seen parents in my school, moved by something that has happened, brush away their tears and try to suppress their emotion entirely. I don't approve. I think they're denying the children around them a look at what it is to be human. What better way to begin developing a sense of caring for others than to allow children to share a sense of the emotions that are our common lot as human beings.

A sense of playfulness

It's a sense of playfulness that we also need to bring into the process. My fifth test for whether an activity is worth doing, you will recall, is whether it can inspire giddy, silly behavior. In February, close to Valentine's Day, I taught the children this poem:

> Pucker your lips,
> Close your eyes,
> You're going to get
> A big surprise.

For days I heard in all corners of the school the poem being repeated and then the "gales of laughter" that meant to me that the poem passed the test. Some of the children, in an unintentional triumph for my second test, expanded on the poem by saying, "Stand on one leg. *Now* pucker."

During February, I greeted my children each morning with the "pucker poem" or a similar love rhyme: "Do you love me or do you not? You told me, but I forgot!"

A sense of playfulness and fun is a wonderful way of feeling close. Think of your favorite bedtime rhymes: "Good night, sleep tight; don't let the bedbugs bite! But if they do, take off your shoe and beat them till they're black and blue!"

I remember demanding another story as a child and my mother saying,

> I'll tell you a story
> About Jack and Nory
> And now my story's begun.

> I'll tell you another
> About Jack and his brother
> And now my story is done.

All adults have favorites and will remember these playful chants all their lives, passing them on to their own children as family tradition.

Sometimes a sense of play can arise quite unexpectedly. This summer, I was teaching a children's workshop on art and music. I was sitting quietly, when John started to decorate me—with sticky dots, cellophane eyes, paper crowns, and ribbons. The rest of the children joined in. (Fortunately, no one thought of the stapler.) What a wonderful, creative project! A week later, they were still talking about it. "Wasn't that great! The day we decorated you?" Yes, it was. It was playful, silly, wonderful fun!

Retaining our own sense of playfulness and wonder means that we will be able to instill in future generations a sense of wonder, a sense of humor, a sense of compassion, a sense of optimism about life and living—a sense that we surely need if we are to survive.

A sense of wonder

the first test: identity and positive self-concept

Try to look back to your own childhood and to remember what made you happy. It will usually have been time — time your parents, grandparents, extended family spent with you. When my grandson Jacob comes to visit, he never wants a new toy: he wants to be the center of my attention for a few hours. He wants to talk, laugh, run in the grass, pick marigolds. He wants to help me cook, to be read to, to be sung to.

The most important thing an adult can do to give a young child a positive self-concept is to give time. In many families today, both parents work. Parents must give careful thought to what really matters to children. Reading about child development, buying every new toy in the store, providing a child with every set of "wheels" from the age of two is not enough ultimately to make a child happy. Children need to be helped to discover what is right and what is appropriate, and they must be helped to develop standards. The most hard-to-provide element in today's family is time.

A gift of time

Like all grandparents, I've spent a good deal of money on toys for my grandchildren. They are very appreciative, but I recently gave Jacob a not-very-extravagant present that is the most treasured gift he has right now—a large box of the new flexible Band-Aids®. He guards them carefully, hiding them in a new spot every day. Very occasionally he shares one with his sister Kylie if she's really hurt. When the Band-Aids® are gone, Jacob's treasure will be the box, I'm sure.

If I were to do a survey and ask a hundred children what makes them happy, I know the answers would be like Jacob's, simple, joyful things that cost adults little but time. At our school, we often talk about our favorite things—what makes us happy—and when I do Mother's Day cards and Father's Day cards, I ask the children, "What's the best thing your mom or dad does?" The answers range from "A hug," to "When Dad plays crazy with me." From "Buying ice-cream cones," to "When my grandpa brought me a cardboard box to play in." What makes children happy? "I like to go to the park and run." "I like Band-Aids®."

positive attention in public places

Every parent knows that being with young children is not an eight-to-five job. Part of the total approach to living with a young child and encouraging language, independence, and self-esteem is being with the child in public and keeping it a positive experience.

First of all, remember that children would rather not be in places that confine them — places where they cannot run, speak loudly, and play. Whenever possible, I think parents should exchange babysitting rather than take children to places where they must stand in lines. This is, of course, not always feasible.

I am often saddened and sometimes appalled at parental behavior in grocery stores, department stores, restaurants, and banks. There are ways to make even these situations more positive experiences for children. First, talk to your child, no matter what the child's age, and explain where you are going. Always have a bag of special things in your car, and always include a favorite book. When babies can sit up, they will love to look at one of those cloth books or special hard books they can't tear. Also in this special bag should be paper, crayons, water-based felt pens, and sticky dots. These few items can save your sanity in the doctor's office, in a line at the bank, in a restaurant. Add a new book or something special occasionally. You must realize that you'll have to keep an eye on the coloring in the beginning. Start with large pieces of paper; you can roll them to save space.

Although my children are now grown, I never leave home without a bag of paper and some crayons. When I wait in line and see a child being cajoled, pulled at, and nagged—or even if the parent is being extremely patient but the child is bored—I offer a piece of paper and a choice of crayons to the child. I think this should be conducted as a national campaign!

If you are in public with a fretful child, don't ever be embarrassed to sing softly —or loudly! Music is soothing. And realize how much joy you might bring to others!

My daughter, Julie, who was herself very impatient as a young child, is a model of patience with her children, especially in the grocery store. She takes the time to tell both her young children and her new baby about the produce; she shows them leeks, kiwi fruit, red potatoes. Sometimes they buy special vegetables, sometimes not, but her gentle and consistent way of making them part of the environment encourages their interest. I find it interesting that unlike many young children, they always seem ready to try new tastes.

One of the best friends you can have for the time you spend in public with your child is a sympathetic librarian or bookstore manager. There are bookstores much closer to me than my favorite, but I consider the drive worth it. The staff knows the latest in children's books; they will always order any book I request; they'll send a book to my home any time. Just as I feel strongly about greeting people warmly in the school, they feel strongly about greeting their customers. Young parents would do well to develop a relationship with this kind of bookstore, as well as with the children's staff at their local public library.

positive attention in the school

Very often the first few minutes of the school day set the pace for the entire day. I try to sit at the door, on a small chair, and I talk to each child as the children come in. Our children come to school in car pools, so they often arrive at about five-minute intervals. But sometimes they do arrive eight or nine at a time. It is difficult to keep my wits about me when five are clamoring for attention, but this, I think, is one of the most important times of the day.

I've observed the greeting process at other schools. The children run in with concern and anxiety in their eyes until they see the teacher. By sitting at the door, the teacher gives children the assurance of an adult presence right away. More important, it is a daily recognition of the child in a strange environment.

I pay particular attention to a child who has had some difficulty adjusting to school or who is having too many conflicts with the other children. I hold that child (if I can), rub the child's arms, speaking softly about what's going on. Sometimes we get a little silly; sometimes the child will have something sad to tell. Sometimes the child makes things up.

An experience I had this year reminded me that children are very aware of the importance of a daily greeting. I had met the children at the door and already moved to the art area and from there outside, when Adam, whose best friend Elizabeth had just arrived about twenty minutes late, came running out to get me. "Quick, Teacher Bev, Elizabeth is here! Come and say good morning!"

Giving positive attention

Overall, a kiss, a hug, four or five words to each child make the day start right. It is very important to give young children positive attention before a demand for negative attention starts. They all want and need my attention and caring, and I feel that by giving positive attention I avert many problems before they begin.

When I have a new toy or a new book that's special, I have it on my lap so I can share this wonderful new thing with the child. I don't read the book at that time—just share the cover and talk about how nice it will be when story time comes.

Sometimes, in our concern for the child, we try too hard. We need to let the child set the pace and try not to bombard the child with questions. Sometimes just sitting, holding the child's hand or rubbing the child's arm or back will be enough to encourage a conversation. Sometimes words are not necessary. The teacher's presence at the door gives the child the message, "You are important to me. I care about you."

Although mornings with young children — and even older children — are hectic, parents should remember that a few seconds of affection like a rub, a hug, or a few words as the parent wakes the child can really set the pace for the day. When children come home, just a pat, a smile, and a "How was your day?" can make the world seem right. It's tough surviving a day out in the world; just the fact that your child has made it in one piece is deserving of your recognition and appreciation.

options

Most parents as well as teachers would agree that independence is one of the things we want our children to achieve. We must encourage independence very early, allowing children to make the decisions they are capable of making —what to wear to school, for example. Once that choice is offered and acted upon, a parent's apology for a child's appearance—"He dressed himself," for example—negates the whole process.

Growing to independence

Be sure that all the options you present are suitable for the child and acceptable to you. Then allow your child to grow into independence by making choices: using the front door rather than the back door to come into the house; sleeping on the floor rather than in her bed if she wants to; eating a tuna sandwich for breakfast instead of cereal, if the sandwich is available; slicking his hair down with water to look like John Travolta, if that appeals to him.

Again, be sure that the options you present are acceptable, and don't confuse them with the use of ultimatum. My favorite story of a use of option gone astray concerns the older child and husband of a friend of mine, who had been advocating that her husband use presentation of choices as a method of dealing with their pre-adolescent son's foot-dragging about household chores. She came home one afternoon to find her son peacefully napping in his room and her husband fuming. "Options!" he snorted. "I told him, 'All right! You have two choices. Either go and cut the lawn right now or go to your room and go to bed!' *Now* what!!"

The advantage of offering choices to young children in a home or school environment is that while children are making these choices, parents and teachers are there to help them—help them develop the control they need. Control must be exercised with absolute fairness and a good deal of restraint. I see, in too many homes and too many schools, excessive restraint. Parents and teachers seem unable to tolerate noise, dirt, mud, runny noses, bare feet. We have quiet times in our school, but we expect dirt and noise (which we call joyful noise) and arguments. At school, we step in and help children when (1) they could hurt themselves; (2) they could hurt others; or (3) they could damage property.

One of the most significant things we do in our school to establish and reinforce identity in our children is to maximize the number of options open to each child. If there are twenty-four activities available, the odds that each child will find something exciting to do go way, way up.

I'll describe our schedule for you; it works very well for us. It gives the children free time to pursue imaginative, developmental play and still provides some time together for all of us—a time for stories, singing, sharing.

9:00 A.M.	Arrival time. Greetings at the door.
9:15–10:25	Free time.

We have many centers set up for the children both indoors and out—a puzzle table, a clay table, two or three creative art areas, a quiet area, a loft, a music area. Outside we have swings, water play (hose, mud hole). We have materials to build bridges, dams, boats; a very large wooden fort to climb and pretend on; lots of free space; and a bike trail. We often take art activities outside as well.

Our children are free to move from inside to outside during free time with no pressure to do any specific tasks. But most of our children do some art every day.

During free time, I take time to write the children's stories, an activity which is presented in the chapter on creating. I do not insist that each child write a story, but when I pick up my clipboard and a pen, at least ten children start

Joyful noise

demanding to be first. One of the reasons for their enthusiasm, I think, is that I read the stories during circle and thus give them credibility as well as individual recognition.

10:25	Cleanup time.
10:30–10:40	Poetry, sharing, fingerplay, movement.
10:40	Snack.
10:55–11:25	Circle, stories, acting out stories, movement, conversation, reading of children's stories written that day, games.

I wish you could be with me for a day or two and discover the magic of circle—of moving along. Young children cannot be expected to sit still for thirty minutes, but by doing so many different activities that all the children can be involved in, we manage to spend an amazing amount of time together.

transition time

Often, people remark on the tightness of our schedule. We get so much done because I don't waste time waiting for everyone to stop talking or for everyone to finish snack and come to circle.

Needing to socialize

Getting the child "down" means "being still" to some people, but I don't think of it that way. In the first place, teachers aren't television sets. In the second place, if the individual child is really the focus, absolute quiet isn't to be expected. I expect the joyful noise; I expect children to march to different drummers. I don't like chaos, and we don't have chaos, but I'm not afraid to let the children go a little, because I know I can get them back. Finally, young children need to socialize; it's damaging to the whole purpose of the preschool experience to interrupt their conversations constantly with negative attention. Statements like "We'll start when you're all quiet," "Susie, you need to sit still," or "John, are you listening?" are better replaced with something to distract the child whose attention we want.

Our school consists of one large room divided into different centers. The children who are still eating snack can hear and see what we're doing at circle,

but I feel strongly that they should not be rushed. I know the rest of the children's attention will be lost if I don't "capture" them within thirty or forty seconds. This is the time that I call, formally, a transition time. Rather than giving a lecture or directions to the game or a prologue to a story, I often just begin by chanting or singing or doing a fingerplay or two.

Many of you remember the old favorite, "One potato, two potato, three potato four, five potato, six potato, seven potato, more," placing one fist on top of the other. It's a good attention getter, and after we chant it once, we do as many variations as the children call out: going up, going down, with our fists on our foreheads, lips, knees, stomachs, quietly, loudly, with no sound at all, on the floor, with our eyes closed.

Jump rope rhymes are short and often involve movement. We use them frequently—without the rope—for transitions.

Another effective chant for starting is a counting chant:

Clap 2-3-4-5-6-7-8
Jump 2-3-4-5-6-7-8
Cluck 2-3-4-5-6-7-8
Run 2-3-4-5-6-7-8
Snap your fingers 2-3-4-5-6-7-8
Push 2-3-4-5-6-7-8
Pull 2-3-4-5-6-7-8
Roll your head 2-3-4-5-6-7-8
Bounce 2-3-4-5-6-7-8

Even if you're doing this as a sit-down activity, if the child's suggestion requires it, get up. When the child says something that seems impossible, try it. When the five-year-old says, "Try it lying on your stomach with your eyes closed holding your breath," try it!

There are many possible variations here. Try doing only five or so; when the children become uninterested, quit and go on to something new.

There are many action stories that children love and many resources for learning these transitional devices. More are presented in the section on movement in the next chapter. The ones I describe later are old standards, but this one is our favorite. You can change the Bear Hunt to a Santa Hunt by climbing to the North Pole, or you can make it a Bunny Hunt at Easter.

the bear hunt

Teacher: Let's go on a Bear Hunt.
Let's walk. *(Slap thighs.)*
Oh, oh. There's a log. Jump over. *(Hands jump.)*
Let's walk. *(Slap thighs.)*
There's a mountain. Everybody climb. *(Hands climb.)*
We're at the top. Everybody look. See if you see a bear. *(Hands to forehead.)*
(Note: If they say they see a bear at this point, don't disagree, even though the story isn't over.)
Slide down the mountain. *(Slide hands down.)*
Oh, look! Tall grass. *(Hands push grass out of the way and out of face.)*
There's a river. Everybody swim. *(Arms swim.)*
Shake yourself off. *(Shake arms.)*
Oh, look! A forest!
What's a forest? Who lives there? *(You'll get many answers—hippos, lions, worms; the "Could be" response is very useful here.)*
What's that big animal over there behind a tree?
A bear!!
Let's go home!
(Repeat above steps in reverse, quickly, as the bear chases you through forest, river, grass, mountain, log.)

sharing

Listening to others and having them listen to you is the heart of the language development process. Children must learn to listen and respond to one another. They must tell about their experiences.

One of the earliest and best ways for children to start developing a sense of who they are is through sharing time. In our school we have sharing, which some people call "Show and Tell," every day. Some teachers moan and groan when I say this, and sometimes even parents don't seem to realize how important this kind of experience is to the development of oral language and self-concept.

We must create time for children to talk. Too often circle times, sharing times, show and tell times are used for teacher verbalization: the teacher uses this time to "teach," and thus we lose the value of the experience. That value is double as far as I'm concerned: sharing encourages children to develop oral language and also to develop a sense of identity. I call each child's sharing time that child's "moment of glory."

Time to talk

The teacher with a little enthusiasm can make sharing interesting most of the time. Certainly many individual children find sharing the highlight of their day at preschool. Parents often tell me that children wake up in the morning talking about what to take to sharing. They often bring the same thing every day for weeks. It is sometimes their blankets, sometimes little pieces of paper that are so significant to them.

To do daily sharing and maintain everyone's interest, your own sanity, and the child's desire to share some important part of his life with the other children requires a certain attention to technique. While we may focus on the language development happening as children share, for the child the more significant benefit may be being able to get up in front of all the children and having the teacher's total attention for a few seconds.

I mean a few seconds. Your reaction doesn't have to go on for minutes; the child's comments don't need to be extensive. You *do* need to be enthusiastic. Here are some rules for sharing:

(1) Do it with joy in your voice and gesture.

(2) Be sincere. Remember how important this is for the child. It's so easy, when a child has brought her blanket for the hundredth time, to fall into the trap of failing to focus on the child's *feelings* about that all-too-familiar blanket (which may be even easier if the child's

Focus on feelings

parent is standing behind the circle rolling her eyes and muttering, "Oh, my. Not the blanket *again!*"). I might occasionally be a little silly with a child in a situation like this and ask in a mock-suspicious way, "Did you ever bring this blanket before?"

(3) Take advantage of this great time for closeness and touching.

(4) Do the sharing quickly, but don't rush the child. If children seem tense, I hold them or rub their arms or backs.

(5) Change the time you share. We usually share just before a snack, but sometimes I put it off to just before the end of the day. Break up sharing occasionally; share half before snack, half after.

(6) Encourage the children to share experiences as well as objects.

(7) Encourage the children to clap and cheer for each other.

The following exchange, for example, would probably take no more than twelve or thirteen seconds. Brad has brought his blanket to share.

Teacher:	Somebody brought something soft that it's hard to go to sleep without.
Brad:	Me! Me! *(Leaping up)* It's mine!
Teacher:	*(Taking Brad onto lap)* What's the best thing about this blanket, Brad?
Brad:	It's soft—I like it!
Teacher:	Clap and cheer for Brad!
Everybody:	Hooray for Brad! *(Applause)*

clapping and cheering: more positive attention

I encourage applause for all kinds of activities we do—not just for formal situations, like acting out stories. We clap and cheer for participants in games, for each other's art, for snack, for just about everything. I think it's important for children to be shown how to respond positively to each other's efforts.

A teacher attending a workshop of mine this year shared her use of "Standing Ovations," which she encourages her children to ask for if they feel they have done something important. After the child tells everyone what achievement deserves a standing ovation, everyone stands and applauds. What a stroke! Think what a lesson is contained in clapping and cheering, in the standing ovation for the child who is too shy to participate, but who sees over a long period of time that everyone supports each other.

good news, bad news

One day during sharing, Angie jumped up and said, "Teacher, I have good news and bad news to share." She shared her news with us, using the appropriate facial expressions. It was great. Many of the other children immediately demanded equal time to share good news and bad news. This kind of sharing helps young children realize that everything cannot always be the way they want it to be — sometimes a very difficult concept for children, who are, remember, terribly egocentric.

I wouldn't do "Good News, Bad News" every day. Let the children set the pace by proposing the variation or following up with it.

One variation of "Good News, Bad News" I have used is to wander around during free time (when the children are choosing their own activities) and encourage the children to share their good and bad news with me in order to share at circle later. An important point of timing here is to do it *quickly*—and this holds for lists of any kind. Children have short attention spans!

sharing between age groups

In these days of small families, one of the benefits that preschool has to offer children is the opportunity to be with children who are younger and older. I am a little dismayed to see a trend in schools toward age segregation in the early years: the justification for this seems to be that since all three-and-a-half-

New dimensions

year-olds are supposed to be achieving certain developmental goals, it's easier to achieve the goals if you have only three-and-a-half-year-olds to deal with.

I would want to remind my colleagues who are in schools going in this direction of the problems created by an age-segregated approach in the primary grades. The theory is fine: the reality is that the theoretical three-and-a-half-year-old doesn't exist: she may be closer to two-and-a-half; he may be more like four. Why has it been considered progressive and desirable, in the primary grades, to have open classrooms? Because open classrooms recognize that individual children are quite different—and don't penalize them for their differences. The same holds true for younger children.

There are further benefits to working with a mix of ages: it forces the school to be child-centered so that all activities can be performed by children at their own levels. What about the child who because of his late birthdate is in a preschool for three years (over half the child's life so far)? Will boredom or behavior problems result? Not necessarily. In art, what the child has done in prior years takes on new dimensions. More control goes into painting strokes; more thought goes into choosing color; more perception goes into sculpture. During playtime, the older child often organizes the play; very often, the older child will be the "boss." During music time, the confidence of the older child grows because of knowing all the words. The older child masters rhythm— often wants to choose the song. During circle, the older child's attention span is longer. If a story is acted out, the older child needs little direction; often, the older child wants to direct!

sharing through observation

This kind of sharing of activity is excellent for the younger children in the group. Very often, the two-and-a-half-year-old is very tentative about joining in. That's fine! We had one young child who spent much of the first two months of the program under the play table, peeking out. Parents kept trying to coax him into the mainstream until I stopped them. He needed to be under that table—or he wouldn't have been under there. Observing all the activity around him helped that child orient to all the activities in ways that he could not have observed without the presence of older children.

Finally, older children are often very concerned and protective toward younger children. What a marvelous experience for them, especially if they have no younger siblings or no younger neighbors. We define ourselves by reference to other people; I have always believed that a significant part of self-identification in children lies in their relationships to other children—younger and older as well as children of the same age.

the second test:
changing and exchanging

The first of my tests for materials and activities has focused primarily on the need young children have to identify themselves positively as individuals, especially as that need relates to fostering their language development. This chapter deals with a second test for worthwhile language-development materials: do stories, songs, simple movement activities lend themselves, after their initial presentation, to manipulation and change by the child?

Such manipulation is one of the best ways to build vocabulary and to expand thinking. To foster language development, we must be alert to each moment. Children are open for new learning only at very brief intervals—always on their internal schedules, never on ours. By using material that the child can vary, we also avoid that worst of teaching situations in which the child and the material are in the same room at the same time but never connect. If the child is able to create a variation on a basic pattern, that act is proof that some kind of connection has been made.

It takes some work to create an environment in which children will respond to materials in this way. From the first day of school, all of our children are encouraged to participate verbally during story time—to ask questions and to say how they feel about characters or events in the story. Everything they say is accepted; sometimes children present opposing points of view. I always allow ample time for expression from the children before saying, "Let's see what happens."

Picking up cues

One of the simplest ways of encouraging children to change material is by asking them a question you've derived from a song or story you've been doing. If possible, it's best to pick up cues for these questions from the children themselves. You must pay close attention; sometimes the cue is nothing more than a small voice that says at the end of a song or book—in this case Watty Piper's *The Little Engine That Could**—"If I could ride that train, I'd visit my grandpa in San Francisco!"

Almost every child has a favorite destination or a favorite someone to visit. Now, all you need to do is ask! "If *you* could ride that train, where would you like to go?"

During Dinosaur Week, an event we do annually because children are so fascinated with dinosaurs, I asked, "If you had a dinosaur, where could he take you?"

"To see Santa."

"To Grandma's."

"To the moon."

"To the sun and back."

"To Texas."

"To see the whole world."

Learning to listen

What could be more valuable in terms of communication than children sharing places they'd like to go, things they love, ways they like to move, what they'd like to be when they grow up? A valuable process emerges quite naturally in the course of their answering these questions: they are learning to listen, to take turns, to begin conversing with others.

* Full references for books and recordings are given in Chapter 7.

After we read Jill Murphy's *Peace at Last* I asked all the children, "Where do *you* go to find peace and quiet?" The answers were as varied—and honest—as the answerers:

"Under my bed."

"In the closet."

"Out in the barn."

"In the car."

"In Mom's room."

In my tree."

"I don't know where to go, but my mom goes in the bathroom."

And finally, from the lone dissenter, "I don't *like* peace and quiet!"

Asking the right question isn't always dependent on changing a book or story, of course. We bought a family of tiny dolls in a basket; I've been told they're called "worry dolls" or "trouble dolls." I asked the children what they would tell the doll.

"I'm afraid of the dark."

"I can't sleep without my blanket."

"My shoelaces broke and they lost their color."

"There's a snake under my bed."

"My shoes are wet."

"I don't like flies."

"My horse can't sleep in my bed."

"Loud noises hurt my ears."

Another day, when we couldn't go out, I started a conversation about how difficult it must be for children to sit still because they have so much energy, acknowledging their need to run, yell, play and, as we say in our school, "be crazy." Immediately, one child called out, "I'm saving my energy!" What followed was a marvelous conversation in which all the children shared what they were saving their energy for.

"For playing."

"For the next day it doesn't rain."

"To drive a tractor."

"For hunting Easter eggs."

"To go see a whale."

"I'm saving mine, and when I get home, I'm going to jump on Mom's bed!"

Because we have parents actively participating in our program, we're able to record the responses as they come. Sometimes we duplicate the answers to send home to parents, just to let them know what's been going on in the children's minds. Often, however, the next time we read a book or sing a song that has involved this list of answers to a question, the children themselves will ask me to read what they said last time; then, most often, they'll offer a *new* response—an answer that reflects how *they've* changed!

once-upon-a-time stories

We have available for our children three or four homemade books that we call "Once-Upon-a-Time" stories. The importance of these stories is, again, that they encourage children to use language freely. Parents should consider making up a few of these for use in the home as well: children will read them over and over.

You'll need construction paper or some other heavy paper, like tag paper, and pictures of your choice. One of our most popular choices is the "Growth Story," for which you'll need pictures of babies of different ages and stages. The cover of the book says, "Once upon a time . . ." And the first page says, "You were a baby," next to an appropriate newborn picture. The remaining pages don't need words, just pictures of babies growing and changing. Twelve

to fifteen pictures are plenty. We end our books with pictures of preschool-age children, but certainly the books could go on and on.

We read these stories during circle and encourage lots of verbalization. "Do you think this baby can talk? Walk? *Now* what can he do?"

Many of our preschoolers have siblings, so they have much to say about infant growth—much of which is about what the babies *cannot* do. If you make these books available in your reading area and listen, you'll hear wonderful conversations about babies. A variation of this kind of "no-word" book involves clipping all kinds of pictures and saving them so that more than one child can make a book.

changing songs

I believe absolutely in the value of music in education for its own sake (see Chapter 6), but the role music plays in offering materials for children to manipulate and vary is invaluable to language development in the preschool program. We do many songs, of course, that don't easily suggest change; I have presented some songs we do for their own sake in Chapter 6; but many of our favorites have built-in opportunities for children to change verses and choruses—again, demonstrating that they have made the original their own.

In encouraging children to make up materials to familiar songs, don't be concerned with your own expectations. Don't be concerned with rhyme—or anything—more than with the children's creating. It's the joy of the children making music—and then making it their own—that's most important. If you've never used this activity regularly and extensively, you're in for a lot of fun!

The activity can be as simple as changing a word or two in an already-familiar song, or it can be adding a verse to an already-familiar rhyme. A five-year-old, when we had finished "Humpty Dumpty" one day, jumped up and recited his version:

Humpty Dumpty sat on the wall
Humpty Dumpty had a great fall
All the King's horses and all the King's men
Had scrambled eggs for breakfast.

aiken drum

There is an old favorite—Scottish, I think—called "Aiken Drum," that the children love because we can make up additional verses.

There was a man lived in the moon,
Lived in the moon, lived in the moon,
There was a man lived in the moon,
And his name was Aiken Drum.

And he played upon a ladle,
A ladle, a ladle.
And he played upon a ladle,
And his name was Aiken Drum.

Second verse: **And his hat was made of cream cheese.**

Third verse: **And his coat was made of good roast beef.**

Last year, in one of our invented versions, his pants were made of French bread, and one of the children said, "Now we have a sandwich," so we sang, "And now we have a sandwich, a sandwich, a sandwich . . . and it is very good."

I am always amazed at how creative children can be; each year we seem to expand on old favorites in new ways. This year, I began "Aiken Drum," and after the first verse and chorus, I asked what his head was made of.

"A potato," a child shouted.

I asked a parent to grab the crayons and a large sheet of paper, and she began to draw the children's answers. His hair was spaghetti; his eyes were made of strawberries; his nose of cheese—Swiss, of course; and his mouth was made of chocolate kisses.

Aiken
Drum

We have since sung "Aiken Drum" dozens of times, always asking one of our parents to draw Aiken, and although we've hung all of these versions on the wall, none of them have ever been the same.

worried man

Another folk favorite that provides children with the opportunity to create their own words is "It Takes a Worried Man to Sing a Worried Song." After we sing it, I say, "What's worried? What does worried mean?"

Sometimes what emerges is a very short conversation. Sometimes we all share something to worry about. I'm always amazed that young children know so many emotions to verbalize about. Think of the possibilities—children conversing about crying, laughing, affection, anger.

If you want to vary the activity, you can encourage the children to stand in front of the group and demonstrate the emotion they want to sing about. Some will be a little shy and want to do it from your lap or from their chair or position on the floor. That's fine!

One day, someone said, "I want to do one, but I don't want to do it with my face."

I said, "All right! Show me how you want to do it."

He sang, as he bent up and down from the waist, "It takes a bent-over man to sing a bent-over song."

Six or seven of the children then came up with new versions: a sideways man, a forward man, a backward man, a clapping man, a jumping man. It was great!

the bus song

The wheels on the bus
Go round and round,
Round and round,
Round and round,

The wheels on the bus
Go round and round,
All around the town.

The wipers on the bus
Go swish, swish, swish,
Swish, swish, swish,
Swish, swish, swish,
The wipers on the bus
Go swish, swish, swish,
All around the town.

What makes this favorite special, again, is that new verses can be added. It is a delightful action song. The lights on the bus go blink, blink, blink. The money on the bus goes clink, clink, clink.

When young children are encouraged to create new verses, it can also be an outrageously silly song: "The cows on the bus go moo, moo, moo"; "The snake on the bus wiggles all around."

Children are so terribly observant! "What about a teacher on the bus?" I asked one day. The response was, "The teacher on the bus says, 'Please sit down, please sit down.'"

other favorites

Other songs that lend themselves to creative tampering with/by young children are "Down by the Bay," "When I Was a Lady," "The Bear Went Over the Mountain," and that perennial favorite, "Don't Throw Your Junk in My Back Yard." "The Peanut Song" suggests endless variations, and "The More We Get Together" combines new verses with new movement.

down by the bay

Down by the bay (down by the bay)
Where the watermelons grow
  (where the watermelons grow),
Back to my home (back to my home)
I dare not go (I dare not go).
For if I do (for if I do)
My mother will say (my mother will say),
"Did you ever see a bee
With a sunburned knee
Down by the bay?"

Repeat first six lines to:

"Did you ever see a cow
With a green eyebrow
Down by the bay?"

"Did you ever see a moose
With a loose tooth
Down by the bay?"

Whales with pails

It's only the beginning. Our children have produced a whale with a pail, a dad being sad, a goat in a boat, a pig in a wig, a bean wearing jeans. Rhyming isn't necessary, of course, but often they'll want to try.

the bear went over the mountain

Oh, the bear went over the mountain,
The bear went over the mountain,
The bear went over the mountain,
To see what he could see.

To see what he could see,
To see what he could see,
Oh the bear went over the mountain
To see what he could see.

The children can vary both where the bear went and what he saw when he got there. Again, sometimes they will attempt rhyme, sometimes not. Either, of

down by the bay

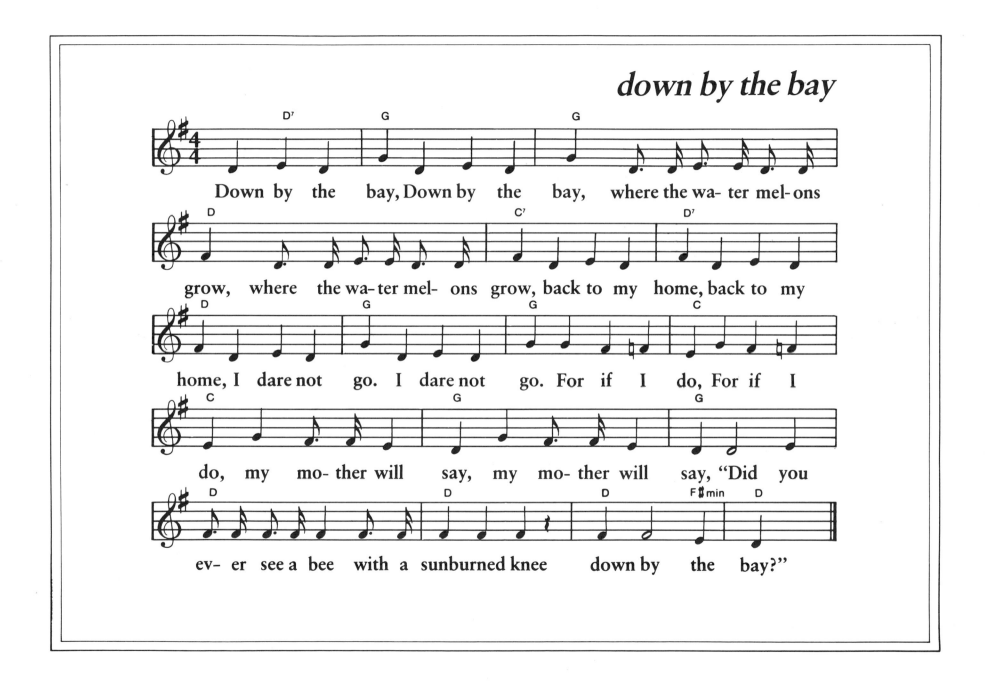

course, is fine. If you try this, you might get a bear who went down the road and eventually saw a toad. More suspensefully, we have had a bear who went into my bedroom and saw "—not me! I'm under the covers!" and a three-part effort about a bear who went to a local supermarket, saw all the honey, and ate it all up.

when I was a lady

When I was a lady,
A lady, a lady,
And when I was a lady,
A lady was I.

And this way and that way
And this way and that way,
And when I was a lady,
A lady was I.

The variations are as simple as asking the children, "Now what would you like to be?" Often it's the people they see around the preschool—"When I was a train driver," "A telephone fixer," "A garbage collector.

don't throw your junk in my back yard

Don't throw your junk in my back yard,
My back yard, my back yard,
Don't throw your junk in my back yard,
My back yard's full!

We talk about our back yards first, and I encourage the children to think about what they don't want there. All children will have reasons for not wanting certain things in their back yards. Last year a little girl didn't want raisins in her back yard because she hated them. On an earthier note, a little boy started his statement by explaining, "Well, we have three dogs in our back yard." Everyone knew immediately what he didn't want any more of in *his* back yard.

the peanut song

Pea- nut sit-ting on the railroad track, heart was all a-

flutter! Down the track came a railroad train. Oh, Oh! Peanut butter!

don't throw your junk in my back yard

Don't throw your junk in my back yard, my back yard, my back yard!

Don't throw your junk in my back yard! My back yard's full!

the peanut song

Peanut sitting on the railroad track,
Heart was all a-flutter,
Down the track came a railroad train,
Oh, Oh! Peanut butter!

We have begun with a banana (to a banana split), a tomato (to catsup or juice), an apple (to sauce or cider), but my favorite was the child who began with a marshmallow and ended, "Oh, oh! A mallow mess!"

the more we get together

The more we get together,
Together, together,
The more we get together,
The happier we'll be.

For your friends are my friends,
And my friends are your friends.
The more we get together,
The happier we'll be.

Children suggest almost immediately, "The more we clap together," "The more we laugh together," "The more we yawn together," "The more we jump together." A group of twenty-four children will produce twenty-four new movements out of this song—if the activity sustains their interest that long.

Sometimes you will plan a song and be surprised by the variations the children will find possible. "I Know an Old Lady Who Swallowed a Fly" was subject this summer to a different kind of variation than I had ever experienced; what the children in my summer workshop did to it is a good illustration of the principle that variations don't have to be expected or even follow the same pattern as the song.

When I had finished reading the story and singing the song to the group, John said, "I know an old lady who swallowed John. He was gone when she swallowed John."

That did it. Each child had to have a rhyming turn. Sometimes, the rhyme didn't make sense, but the children were experimenting with language and having fun. We had the old lady "swallowing Becky out on the decky," and we didn't quibble with the old lady who "swallowed Sarah. Oh, what a barah!"

commercials

I hope you can sense that some of the most successful songs for young children are those that allow the children to create their own verses. I have also had great success with television commercials: "I wish I were an Oscar Mayer wiener" produces great variations. "Chun King for your beautiful body" becomes "Try jumping (or a hundred movements) for your beautiful body."

I wouldn't pretend, in spite of my mistrust of television in the lives of young children, never to watch it or to claim that children shouldn't ever watch it. Certainly when we use television materials in such a way that children can manipulate them, we are counterbalancing the passivity that television is said to produce in children. We show children that they can create from what they see—that, in fact, they can control it. This is a very important lesson; I don't encourage books to be regarded as untouchable or somehow sacred, either.

Counterbalancing passivity

Sometimes you will need to suggest a direction in first presenting materials. For the Oscar Mayer wiener presentation, for example, ask children to think about what kind of animal they'd like to be—and why! Then the song might go like this:

> I wish I were a great big bear,
> That is what I'd truly like to be.
> For if I were a great big bear,
> Everyone would be afraid of me!

"Reach Out and Touch Someone" can be varied at the end. "This time," I tell the children, "we're not going to say, "Hi," but what we'll say or do."

"Sometimes you feel like a nut; sometimes you don't" has become "Sometimes you feel like a jump; sometimes you don't." We not only deserve a break today, according to our children, but kisses and bumps, and it is not only my dog that might be better than your dog, but my arm, my hand, my laugh.

One final note: all of us have observed the child who doesn't sing during music time, but just listens. It is important not to pressure the young child in this situation. Very often, I've had parents tell me that this child has learned all the words and is singing the songs at home. When I'm getting ready to sing, I often say, "What's something Teacher doesn't like to do alone?" They all answer, "Sing!" I don't preach for half an hour about it. My attitude is that they'll all sing. Sooner or later, most of them do.

movement

The expressions "creative dance" and "creative movement" are confusing to many parents and teachers. They sound a little high-flown. They're not at all. They represent a very simple range of activities that children in a good environment would be doing anyway. Young children are still becoming aware of their bodies—what they are able to do physically—and their coordination skills are developing. Movement is an important part of a program for the developing child, but it is most important to remember that while movement encourages development of balance, rhythm, concentration, cooperation, discovery of space, and coordination, we must consider self-esteem and individual effort the primary goals of movement. Movement has the additional benefit of allowing children to volunteer and demonstrate variations of the basic material.

In the beginning, be specific. Stamp your feet, clap your hands, bounce on your bottom, shake your hand, shake your other hand, stretch high, bend, swing, shake all over. Children need to learn in a very positive, upbeat way what they can do with their bodies. Many children will only observe at first, while others will move or dance right away.

As their confidence grows, try new movement ideas: clap in a specific rhythm, and encourage one child to demonstrate a clap and have the others copy. Do not expect complicated clapping rhythms.

name games

Try clapping names out by syllable. Start with first names if the children are very young. Then progress to first and last names and let each child clap his or her name. Sometimes we do our names to movement as well. As I say, "Bev Bos," for example, I might stamp for Bev and sweep my hand for Bos.

After a child demonstrates a name, have everyone copy. Don't pressure three- and four-year-olds; if they don't quite get the idea about syllables, I don't make a point of teaching them on the spot! You most be careful to keep this activity moving along; don't allow it to drag!

music and movement

Strauss's "*Feuerfest* Polka" with its intriguing use of bells is just one example of a marvelous movement to music. I have the children move, in their own ways, to this wonderful polka, not bumping into others, until they hear a bell. They must listen for the bells and then jump or clap when they hear the bell.

This summer, I had a large class of children who were unable to go outside because of the facility we were using; I sensed they needed to move, put on the *Feuerfest*, and they jumped on cue. When I started the record again, a six-year-old said, "This time, no jumping! Put both arms in the air!"

And the next time, they twirled around at the sound of the bell. The most marvelous part of the activity was that *all* the children in a range from three to eight participated.

Strauss's "Champagne Polka" has wonderful cymbals that can be used in the same way; the "Pizzicato Polka" is another light, quick selection that can be used for many movement activities.

I will later talk about Rossini's "Overture" to *William Tell* as a good selection for musical drawing; it's equally good for movement. Often I encourage the children to keep time by slapping their hands on their legs, softly when the music is quiet, loudly as the volume increases. Sometimes I encourage them to run in place to the music. I frequently find that the entire overture is too long;

try to be sensitive to the moment when it's time to stop a recording. Don't be afraid to interrupt the "performance."

Music can be added to all movement. It's wonderful if you have someone to play the piano, but if you don't, spend some time listening to a variety of music and have it ready. Of course, you can move without music, and I would suggest that you do it both ways. The most important thing, again, is to set up the activity so that the child can change the ending, modify the chant, suggest a new way to do it. Always ask after the first verse, "How else can we do this?" If the children are hesitant, say, "Do you think we could go up?" If a child says, "Do it on your little toe," try it. Nothing is impossible.

Movement often suggests directions, and directions mean language development. Every day, for a few moments, creative movement should be encouraged. By October of the school year, if you say, "Be a frog," most of your children will move quickly to a position that imitates a frog's. Next time, add, "On a log, log, log." Or another day, say, "Be a frog, frog, frog on a lily pad, pad, pad." Just as children are individual and unique, so are frogs. Expect the frogs to be different.

Children can pretend to be anything: trees—tall trees, trees blowing in the wind, trees with no leaves, trees shivering in the wind, shivering in the snow. They can pretend to be flowers, growing, bending in the wind, or rain, closed or open. They can be chicks—cracking open their shells; they can be ponies or pumpkins. They can pretend to be on a hot sidewalk. They can be moving in a dark cave.

Pretending to be anything

Make a movement list at the beginning of the year, and keep it on the piano or close by and choose one or two "moving" things a day.

Sample Movement List

Animals:	Bears, lions, monkeys, tigers, elephants, zebras, ponies, horses, cows, giraffes, dogs, kittens, cats, anteaters, alligators, mice.
Birds:	Storks, eagles, buzzards, pigeons, birds flying, birds resting, birds flying down for food.
Fish and Water Animals:	Whales, sharks, trout, goldfish.
Toys:	Toy soldiers, dolls, wind-up toys, balls, tops, boats, airplanes, trains.

Time is an important factor here. Sometimes young children will get very involved in being something; at other times, they'll be through in twenty seconds. When the children are through for the moment, move on. Try another movement or movement game.

movement game: follow me

You'll need music for this game: Hap Palmer's *The Feel of Music* or *Movin'* would be especially good. If you play the piano, you'll have to be prepared to play a variety of rhythms—fast, slow, varying beats. I prefer recorded music for this game just because it's easier. Any music is appropriate, but a variety of tempos is what you're after.

Pick one child to be the first leader. Listening to the music, the child will move in any way he or she feels. The other children are to imitate the leader. After forty or fifty seconds, I suggest, "You may choose the next leader." Repeat this process until as many children have had a turn as want one.

No rigid rules

I talked earlier about non-verbal communication; this game is a marvelous example. There's no right or wrong here, no rigid rules. Their moving is as varied as the colors of wildflowers: some children will move only one finger to the music; others will move their whole bodies. Each child can express feelings about the music in an individual way.

More important, the children are building the kind of self-confidence that will facilitate getting up in front of a group and speaking. Muscle development and hand-eye coordination are factors here, but these are secondary to the development of self-awareness and self-esteem that is involved.

Variations of this game involve sitting in a circle with the leader in the middle or pairing children up into teams with leader and follower changing positions once or twice.

grandma's glasses

Here are Grandma's glasses, *(Make glasses with fingers)*

Here is Grandma's cap, *(Make cap with hands and put on head)*

And here's the way she folds her hands and puts them on her lap. *(Fold hands)*

Here's Grandpa's glasses, *(Make bigger glasses)*

Here's Grandpa's big tall hat *(Make tall hat on head)*

And here's the way he folds his arms—just like that *(Fold arms)*.

Variable verses, to be done by individual children and imitated by the group:

Here are your (wild, crazy, purple, sun) glasses

Here is your (huge, ugly, army, ski) hat

And this is the way you fold your arms and put them in your lap.

five little monkeys

We do this as fingerplay but also act it out. The children enjoy the fingerplay, but they love it when we do it as movement:

Five little monkeys, jumping on a bed,
One fell off and bumped her head,
Mama called the doctor, and the doctor said,
No more monkeys jumping on the bed!

Repeat through four, three, two, and one monkeys.

We act it out, choosing five children to jump on an imaginary bed, and then call out a name: "Erica fell off and conked her head." One child is Mama and another is the doctor. You can, of course, do as many monkeys as you like— eight or nine or a dozen—so that everyone will get a turn.

the witch has an itch

This wonderfully silly chant for young children which requires their involvement and ingenuity is also a good transition.

> The Witch has an itch.
> The Witch has an itch.
> Where, oh where, does the witch have an itch?

The children take turns shouting out where we must scratch. Some of the older children get as specific as "the wart on her nose"!

ring around the rosie

We do "Ring Around the Rosie" as both a song and a movement story. It is a marvelous transition activity. We do not, however, do it in a circle. The children stand around at random, and we chant the verse, doing the action, "All fall down." Then we repeat, encouraging the children to change the last line: "All jump up," "All bend over," "All spin around," "All clap our hands," "All snap our fingers," "All shout hooray," "All rest."

> Ring around the Rosie,
> Pocket full of posie,
> Ashes, ashes,
> All fall down!

Variations on the last line don't have to be a movement; they can be sleeping or resting, and they can also be just verbal, such as "All say hello," "All whisper goodbye."

musical friends

The children hop, skip, gallop, or move to music around the room. When the music stops, they will shake hands, hug, or just say "hello" to the child nearest them, and then skip, hop, or gallop again when the music begins.

An easy variation is to have the children sit in a circle—on chairs or on the floor—and have one child move around the circle. When the music stops, the child shakes hands, says "hello," or hugs the nearest child and then trades places with that child.

Suggest a handshake, hug, or "hello" to the child, but always allow the child to suggest alternatives—other than hitting, of course. We've had children bow, kiss, or sometimes just smile or giggle.

show us what to do

In a circle, all children can stand or sit, with one person—a parent, teacher, or child—in the middle. Sing or chant:

> (Mary), show us what to do,
> What to do, what to do,
> (Mary), show us what to do,
> And tell us when to stop,
> And tell us when to stop.

Young children like this game, and I think one of the reasons is that, again, there's no right or wrong way to do it—no pressure to move in exactly one way. The first leader chooses the next leader.

Sometimes, even when you repeat, "and tell us when to stop," a child will go on—jumping and jumping and jumping. Since everyone wants a turn, sometimes you must end that child's turn. I sometimes am able to do this very matter-of-factly by saying, "Pick the next leader, Julie. Whew, that's enough of this movement—pick someone else," or, "That was a good movement, but pick someone else."

moving to song lyrics

Many times, the words of songs lend themselves to movement. Some examples are "Michael, Row the Boat Ashore," "Hush, Little Baby," "It's Raining, It's Pouring" (wiggle fingers in a downward motion), and "One, Two, Buckle My Shoe."

one potato, two potato

Another good transition device, which most adults will remember doing to see who's out or in, this chant can also be a creative movement game for young children. Place fists one on top of the other and chant, "One potato, two potato, three potato, four; five potato, six potato, seven potato, more!" Now that they have the idea, do variations. Remember, if a child says, "We can do it on our thumbs," the proper response is, "Show us how," and then trying it!

jump rope rhymes

There are many jump rope rhymes that are appropriate for movement. Sometimes a little word changing may be necessary, but what I hope to inspire you to see is how to use rhymes and songs that you already know and then make them creative by encouraging the children to suggest a new movement.

Moving to rhyme

In every library there are books of songs and rhymes. Edith Fowke's *Sally Go Round the Sun* is especially fine. Remember to check poetry books, too. Often parents will be a superb resource. Everyone seems to remember a different rhyme, but "Teddy Bear, Teddy Bear" is a good example.

First, chant the rhyme. Be sure to establish a rhythm. After chanting the rhyme once or twice, add a movement.

Teddy Bear, Teddy Bear, turn around.
Teddy Bear, Teddy Bear, touch the ground.
Teddy Bear, Teddy Bear, show your shoe.
Teddy Bear, Teddy Bear, that will do.

Teddy Bear, Teddy Bear, go upstairs.
Teddy Bear, Teddy Bear, say your prayers.

Teddy Bear, Teddy Bear, turn off the light.
Teddy Bear, Teddy Bear, say "Good night!"

Jelly in a bowl
Jelly in a bowl
Wibble, wobble, wibble, wobble
Jelly in a bowl!

Peel a banana upside down.
Peel an orange, round and round.
If you jump to twenty-four,
You can have your turn once more.

Change *jump* to *blink, clap, stomp, shake* (arm, hand, fingers), or to any movement suggested by the children. Also, remember that to jump twenty-four times is too many times for young children. We say, "If you can jump to four or more!"

night walk

Our very favorite movement story may be yours as well. We achieve variation by changing the personnel:

Once upon a time there were a whole bunch of kids, *(Indians, Moms, Dads)*
And they were sleeping outside in the grass, *(Everybody sleeps)*
And they were snoring. *(Snore)*
One person was snoring louder, *(Snore louder)*
But someone was awake, *(You can give this person a name)*
And she (he) smelled smoke,
So she (he) ran on the road, *(Slap thighs)*
Over the bridge, *(Slap chest)*
Over the cobblestones, *(Clack tongue)*
Through the dry, dry dirt, *(Rub hands together)*
Until she (he) came to the forest, and
Yes, There was a forest fire! *(Agitated action)*
So she (he) ran back through the dry dirt, *(Rub hands)*
Over the cobblestones, *(Clack tongue)*
Over the bridge, *(Slap chest)*
On the road, *(Slap thighs)*
And she (he) woke everyone! *(Wake everyone)*
And they all ran on the road, *(Slap thighs)*
Over the bridge, *(Slap chest)*
Over the cobblestones, *(Clack tongue)*
Through the dry, dry dirt, *(Rub hands)*
Until they came to the forest, and

Yes, the forest was on fire! *(Agitated action)*
So back they went through the dry, dry dirt, *(Rub hands together)*
Over the cobblestones, *(Clack tongue)*
Over the bridge, *(Slap chest)*
On the road, *(Slap thighs)*
To get their buckets of water,
And back they went to put the fire out,
On the road, *(Slap thighs)*
Over the bridge, *(Slap chest)*
Over the cobblestones, *(Clack tongue)*
Through the dry, dry dirt, *(Rub hands together)*
But many of the buckets had holes!
So they must run back
Through the dry, dry dirt, *(Rub hands together)*
Over the cobblestones, *(Clack tongue)*
Over the bridge, *(Slap chest)*
On the road, *(Slap thighs)*
And patch the buckets with mud from the river bank
And then fill the buckets and go back to the forest,
On the road, *(Slap thighs)*
Over the bridge, *(Slap chest)*
Over the cobblestones, *(Clack tongue)*
Through the dry, dry dirt. *(Rub hands together)*
When they finally all arrived *(Count to three)*
One-two-three, they all threw the water at once
And put out this huge fire!
And then they all went home
Through the dry, dry dirt, *(Rub hands together very slowly)*
Over the cobblestones, *(Clack tongue very slowly)*
Over the bridge, *(Slap chest very slowly)*
On the road, *(Slap thighs very slowly)*
And everyone went back to sleep
And snored *(Snore)*
Loudly! *(Snore loudly)*

the third test: creating

Children need to know that stories can come from them. To expect a fourth- or fifth-grader to write an essay is futile unless the child has had much previous composing experience. The writing experience can start in the preschool years by letting the child dictate to an adult.

There are many relatively simple ways to foster dictation by the child, but you must be careful with all of them because of the age and inexperience of the child. You must go slowly; you must never pressure the child for answers. You may get only a line or two from some children, but if you don't discourage them, they'll soon be volunteering paragraphs. Never lead a child into the answers you'd like to have.

Encouraging, not leading

If language development is to happen, the answers to questions must be the child's own.

Once upon a time there was a mouse. She lived in a mouse hole. Her name was Jennifer. She had children. Ten children. She fed them soup, sandwiches, and clowns. The clowns were one inch tall. They played with puppets. They went to kindergarten. And they played with Indian dolls.
—Melani, age 4.

stories from pictures

I used to use this activity much more extensively than I now do; I now feel if the child brings a piece of art to me and asks to write a story about it, that the activity is all right. The technique I formerly used—taking paper and felt pens, encouraging the children to draw, and then asking them to tell me about it—probably promoted the idea that drawing in and of itself was somehow incomplete—certainly the last thing in the world I'd want my students to feel!

Sometimes, even when a child originates the idea of writing the story, a little hesitation enters the process. Encourage the child by making a gentle comment, such as "I like that blue." Often this is enough to encourage the child into a response.

"Well, that's the car," the child will offer.

"Is it going anyplace?"

"To the store."

"What kind of store?"

"Grocery."

"Who's driving?"

Hysterical giggling. "I am."

That's it. The story, as you write it, reads: "The blue is a car. It's going to the grocery store. I am driving."

Read the story back to the child to make certain you've written it as the child wanted it. Ask if the story is finished and whether you should write "The End."

Again, I cannot stress strongly enough that you must be scrupulously careful about not leading the child into what you expect or want. For example, when the child said, "To the store," the response might have been to say "Grocery store?" Don't do it!

Storybook by Joye

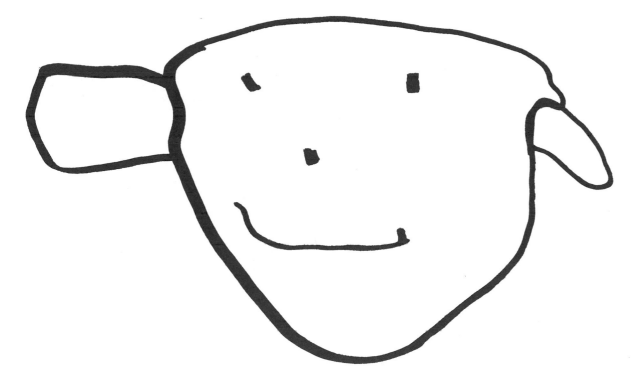

This is teacher. She's reading a book.
It's a good book. It's my book!

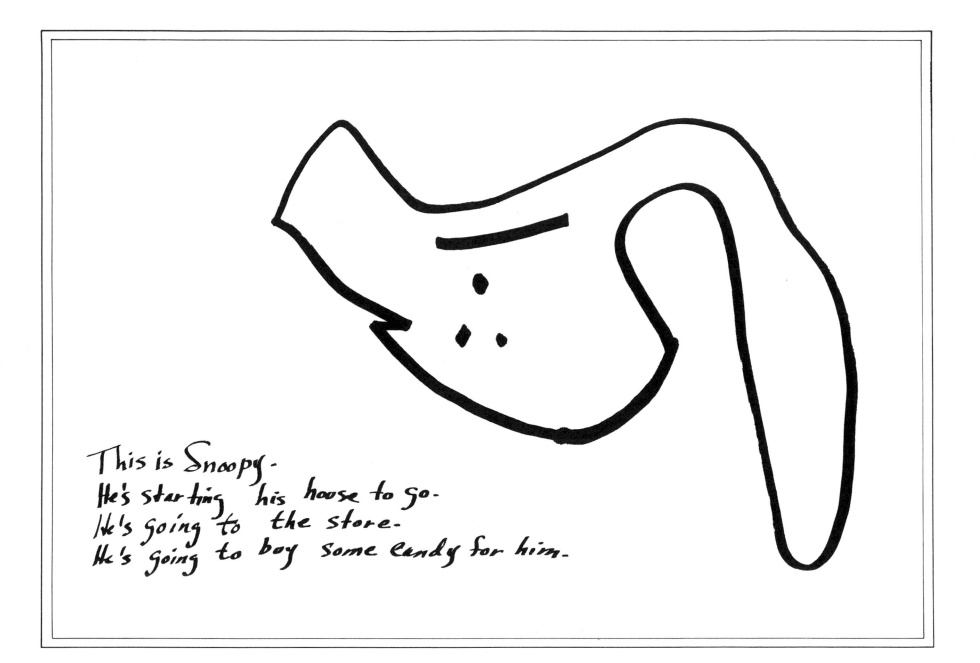

This is Snoopy.
He's starting his house to go.
He's going to the store.
He's going to boy some candy for him.

This is a
bike. It has
training wheels!
It's my bike.
My bike goes fast!

It's a cup! It has
pretend babies on it.
The babies are
crawling. They are
girl babies.
Water is inside the
cup.

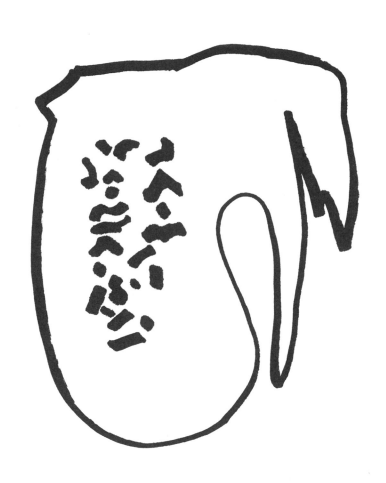

books

By encouraging children to write each day, you will create a situation in which they will begin to want to save all their work in book form. Apart from the fun and satisfaction for the children, this kind of attitude toward books is exactly the sort of introduction children should have to the world of reading.

Sometimes books just happen, with no planning or preparation on my part. During free time, we often do rubbings as one of our art projects, and I encourage the children to take paper and crayons everywhere and rub everything. One day, Josh rubbed all the tires in the back yard and had a dozen or so sheets of paper that read "B.F. Goodrich, 11 × 16," and "Michelin." Another set held tread rubbings. He came to me with the full collection, demanding that I staple them together to make a book.

In any case, you'll need five or six sheets of paper stapled together. As the child begins to tell you a story, turn the page and continue. Sometimes a child will simply expand on the first page. Don't expect a one-day completion of the book. When the child seems ready to move on to other things, say, "I'll keep the book, and you can finish it another day." If the child wants to take the book home, that's all right too!

Once upon a time there was a bear. It wasn't a friendly bear. His name was John. He ate people. He played. He played with his friend bears. He played on the toys that we have. He had clay—same color we have. He rolled the clay dough. He used all the things we use for clay.
—Amy, age 4.

reading the books

We read the books the children write during circle. If we want children to value their stories and we recognize the value of their work, then it must be read to peers. If they've written ten stories, you may not have time, nor can you hold young children's interest long enough to read them all in one day. Instead, read two or three a day. Some children will insist on taking their stories home. Let them.

Parents ought to be sure to read these stories to their children in addition to regular bedtime stories.

Valuing work

Once upon a time there was a hippopotamus. He played with puppets and lions. He eats wolves. He sleeps in bed with childrens. He plays games. He goes swimming. He plays with lions. The hippopotamus goes to jail. He has a key to get himself out. So then he goes to Grandma's house and to Snow White's house. And then he goes to bed. He turns off the light.

—*Tricia, age 3.*

about the author

When we read books from the library and they have an "about the author" paragraph in the book, I read it, sharing with the children information about the writer whose books we enjoy. It is not necessary to do this every time you read a book, but children need to discover that everyone can write books, that authors are people, and that they have families. This process inspired me to try an "about the author" addition to the book projects I do with my children.

After the children write a story, quickly, before they get away, I turn the paper over and say, "Now, tell me about the author." The first time you do this, you may have to do a little explaining. "You are the author of this story; you wrote this story." Keep it low-key; ask questions, but don't lead. Be patient.

I start the "author" by saying, "Her name is Amy Williams. Where do you live, Amy? Who lives with you?"

This will sometimes be enough, but if you sense that the child is still interested and wants to go on, encourage that child by saying, "Tell me some more about you." One question they all love to answer is, "What do you want to be when you grow up?"

The written paragraph would read something like this:

> About the Author: Erica Jones lives in Roseville. She lives with her mom and dad and brother Paul. She is five years old. She wants to be in kindergarten when she grows up.

When I read a child's story during circle time, I also read about the author just as if I were reading a library book. If you could see the faces of three- and four- and five-year-olds, knowing that they can write books that are just as important during circle as any library book!

sticker stories

In variety stores, hobby shops, school supply catalogs and stores, card shops, and even grocery stores, an incredible variety of stickers is available—dino-

Once upon a time there was a fish. He lived in the ocean. It was a big fish. He ate pigs. He sat around all day and watched TV. His name was Cottontail. He goes to preschool. He likes school.

—*Jennifer, age 4.*

saurs, nursery rhyme characters, flowers, holiday stickers, stickers for cultural interests. One packet I bought recently contained bandages, zippers, nuts and bolts, and locks and keys.

Put one sticker on a piece of paper, and have at least five or six pieces for the child to choose from. Some stories can be quite lengthy, so the sheet should be at least twelve by fourteen inches. Be sure to have a few extras on hand in case the child doesn't like any of the choices you have available.

Then proceed as for regular stories and books, above. Remember, as with the other types of stories, don't lead, and don't correct. This is not a test; it is an activity designed to elicit a response from within the child.

biography

The first time you try this will be the most difficult. After the children hear the first one, everyone will want a turn, and they will be much more willing to participate. During circle time, take a piece of paper and a pencil or pen, and start the biography yourself by saying the name of one of the children in the class, such as, "I know a boy named Jonathan. He's four years old." Encourage everyone to participate by adding a line. The special child whose turn it is will often be ecstatic, shaking his head, laughing, and just enjoying the whole procedure. If children have difficulty thinking of something, encourage them —gently—by saying, "You could tell about his clothes or the color of his eyes or hair," or "Do you play with him?" Make the questions general. If a child has great difficulty, it's best to say, "Do you want to think about it, and we'll come back to you?" Make every effort to make this low-key. No child should be embarrassed for not participating.

Once in a while, a child will get silly and say something off-the-wall, such as "He wets his pants." Such comments, of course, are not the end of the world, but when you read the biography back to the children and must repeat the offending line, the listening and enjoyment will stop as every child repeats it ten times. Without making a fuss about it, I say calmly, "I don't want to write that in Jonathan's story. Tell me something else about him." I might even ask the child we're writing about if he wants this line in his story. If you can sense that the child is embarrassed or getting too much negative attention, move on. Say, "We'll come back to you." Again, I must stress, be careful not to fall into the trap of delivering a lecture or giving negative attention.

Be your own judge of a group. Some groups of children won't be able to hold together while you ask twenty-four of them for statements. I don't start these stories until the school year is well established—January, perhaps. If the group would have difficulty sitting through the activity, I "capture" each child during free play time and tell him or her that I'm writing a story about Jonathan and do the story that way. The difficulty here is that some children need to see the person we're writing about, and sometimes I have to take the child by the hand and say, "This is Jonathan."

Why take time to do these stories? Everyone likes to feel special. The expression on each child's face makes all the effort worthwhile. Sometimes I have to hold the "story child" on my lap while I read the results, because the child feels a little self-conscious but still wants that moment of special attention.

Feeling special

Another reason for doing the biographical story is that some children play with only one or two other children during the whole school year. This is quite normal, but they really don't get to know other children. Individual stories provide the focus for getting to know everyone.

From a language development standpoint, biographies are a nice balance for purely imaginative writing. They show children, by example, that stories can be written by looking around at and talking about the real world—in this case, one's classmates and friends.

autobiography

We also encourage the children to write stories about themselves. In a non-pressured way, it encourages awareness about family, friends, neighborhood. We talk about their favorite things—favorite foods, favorite stories. Try to

make this a conversation with the child, not an interrogation. Since children's thoughts and preferences change so quickly at this age, self-stories are always new material.

holiday stories

You'll need holiday cards—lots of them—for this activity. We often acquire Christmas card catalogs from stores and organizations after Christmas. Once you let people know that you want old cards, you'll have hundreds. Be sure to ask for occasional cards as well. You'll need five or six sheets of twelve-by-fourteen-inch paper stapled to make a book.

I tear the picture off the card so it's a single sheet and then put out a good selection of cards in the middle of a table—but not so many as to be confusing to the child. Perhaps a dozen or so is a good number. Encourage the children to pick out three or four cards, glue one card on each page of the book and tell a story.

Any holiday cards can be used with great success. Birthday cards are also fun. If parents are willing, have children bring their birthday cards to school, glue them into a book, and tell about them.

Once upon a time there was a pumpkin that ate paper. And he had strawberry eyes and a cherry nose. He had a dirt mouth. He lived under the mud. His kids and all his family were just the same. They were happy. Their beds were made of cherries and strawberries. The house was made of metal strawberries and cherries. The floor was made out of rocks. That's all.

—Sam, age 5.

the fourth test:
cooperating

Giving children practice in working cooperatively with each other is one of the most important specific functions the preschool has to offer. Practicing cooperation, enjoying cooperation will help the young child immensely — especially in these days of the small family. It isn't only preparation for school that's at stake here, but preparation for all of life.

story time: acting it out

Story time should be the high point of any school day or evening at home, but I have observed that often it is not. Two simple resolutions might make all the difference in your school year or in your reading stories at home, especially if you have more than one child. The first resolution has to do with how you choose stories. The second has to do with a simple procedure we add to nearly all the nursery rhymes, stories, and songs we use—we act out almost everything we do.

First, resolve to choose books for the sheer simple joy of the story. Especially for the very young, stories must be fun! No book should be chosen and read

For the joy of it

with the idea that children are going to learn "how to" or "about" anything at all. In many instances, they may learn something too, but your first consideration must be, "Will they enjoy hearing this?" If you make a mistake, as we all can, and begin to sense their failure to respond, for goodness' sake, put the book down, saying something like, "I don't think this is the right book for today," or "Let's save this book for another time."

Once you have a good book, why resolve to act it out? First, I think because children enjoy the process so very much. But there are many additional reasons for including acting as part of language development activity. Before children read, as we have said before, they need experiences to attach words to. To hear stories is important: it develops listening skills. To have the chance to act out the characters develops further skills — it is the difference for children between being only an audience and being active participants.

Even more important, acting extends children's play. It provides an opportunity for the child to be something different—big, little, brave—to be the boss, to be the baby, to be the teacher, to be whatever the child wants most to be that day.

I like to start the preschool year with nursery rhymes, acting them out. It sets the stage for later acting out of more complicated stories. Many nursery rhymes and fairy tales can be acted out, of course. We love to do "Humpty Dumpty" and "Jack and Jill." The "Three Billy Goats Gruff" is one of the very best. If we did it once a week, our children would never tire of it. "Little Miss Muffet" is also one of our favorites. I have observed that as late as February, I can say, "Let's do 'Miss Muffet,'" and the clapping and cheering are as intense as they were in September.

For "Miss Muffet" you'll need a small chair, a margarine container, and a plastic spoon. As you recite, Miss Muffet sits in the middle of the circle, eating the curds and whey. Another child will be the spider. It's so hard to wait until "Along came a spider" that sometimes the spider will start creeping along the floor before we even begin the rhyme. Miss Muffet, of course, is horribly frightened, throws the dish and spoon away, and runs back to her place.

One of the most enjoyable variations on "Miss Muffet" I have discovered is that after all the children have had a turn, I always sit in the little chair and, without telling the children what to do, start reciting the rhyme. Of course, since there is no chosen spider, all twenty-four of them creep up to scare me. The children enjoy this very much.

As with every activity, there are some traps to watch out for in acting out stories. I think we sometimes provide too many props and visual aids. Don't overdo; children have marvelous imaginations. Try to give every child a turn. Nobody will want to wait until tomorrow, so plan ample time so that you can repeat. Everyone will want to be the spider. I handle this in several ways. Obviously, boys can pretend to be girls when acting; an actor can pretend to be anything. We talk about this well ahead of time. Thus, the boys can be Miss Muffet.

I also encourage participation by promising to act out the rhyme another day. No child, of course, is coerced into participating. We need children to clap and cheer, too. Usually the enthusiasm of all participants is so great that they don't care what they are just as long as they can be something.

Once you start encouraging the children to act out stories, they will be so enthusiastic they'll want to act out everything you read. Many children's books lend themselves well to acting—and children see possibilities that we might miss. One day I read Pat Hutchins's delightful *Don't Forget the Bacon* and barely got the last word out of my mouth when Josh screamed, "I wanna be the bacon, I wanna be the bacon!" I must add, for those of you who haven't read the book, that there isn't any bacon; it is the forgotten shopping item. But when we acted it out, Josh played the bacon, waiting to be remembered. It took lots of patience. He was finally forgotten, and we clapped and cheered for the bacon, too!

You will develop a feeling about what stories will be good for acting out. Stories where all the characters are important and have something to do are good. Sometimes there will be too much dialogue for young children, but toward the end of the school year, when many children are approaching five, stories with more dialogue can be attempted. In these cases, be prepared to do more prompting. Because everyone wants a turn the first day, it's nice if the story has between five and ten characters; that way four "repeats" will get everyone a turn. The fairest way of choosing, by the way, seems to be the

When everyone wants a turn

standard going around the circle. You may find stories, though, like Mercer Mayer's *There's a Nightmare in My Closet,* that have only a few characters and are still wonderful to act out. You will need to experiment. Some years we'll have great success with a particular story, and the next year the same story won't work at all.

One of my favorite books for acting out is Carl Sandburg's *The Wedding Procession of the Rag Doll and the Broom Handle and Who Was in It.* The rag doll is marrying the broom handle, and a grander wedding procession will never be possible. Who marches? The Spoon Lickers, the Tin Pan Bangers, the Chocolate Chins, the Dirty Bibs, the Clean Ears, the Easy Ticklers, the Musical Soup Eaters, the Chubby Chubs, the Sleepyheads.

The first day, read the story. Expect a lot of conversation when the story is over about who they'd like to be. Most preschoolers will change their minds at least three times. The second day, go over the story and let the children choose their parts. This process is not easy. Have the book ready; start with the first page and proceed in order. The third day, assemble all props, line up the players, play an appropriate record or piano march, and begin!

For heaven's sake, be flexible. If you have all Chocolate Chins and no Chubby Chubs, what's the difference! Remember that you will also need an audience to clap and cheer—exactly the role for the child or two who won't want to participate by acting. Finally, remember that the procession is for the children, not for an audience of parents. Be relaxed. Have fun!

Another of my favorites is *When I First Came to This Land* by Oscar Brand. This book has delighted my children for years. I often give copies as gifts. It is especially appropriate around Thanksgiving when we talk about Pilgrims. It makes the setting and development of the land so much clearer to young children. And it rhymes. Children love the repetition in this book as well.

This book is also wonderfully illustrated. The first time I "do" this book, I just sing it (the music is printed in the back), and then the second round—usually the next day—we talk about each page. Each page is a chapter in the immigrant's life. We see how the immigrant changes the land, how he builds his house, where he got the wood, how he chopped down some trees, planted others. The immigrant has only a few tools when he comes to the land—an ax, a frying pan, a few utensils—and the children like to look these over and talk

about all the immigrant did with only his "power in the arm," but the book can be loved and enjoyed without any props.

I usually act out the peripheral experience for this book rather than the text itself. In order to act out *When I First Came to This Land,* we begin with a drama about what it must have been like for the immigrant to come to the new land in the ship. With everyone seated on the floor, we talk about the stormy seas, putting lots of movement and action into this drama—seasickness, what the ship is made of, how it moves, blowing hard, rocking violently, then softly as the sea becomes calm. We talk about food and water on the voyage, encouraging the children to expand on the experience, even if they aren't accurate. We sight land. We cheer; we clap. We even kiss the ground to show our joy at finding the new land. We also discuss why the people wanted to leave the old land. Sometimes the discussion will progress into some contemporary thoughts on moving. All of this, of course, is oral language development.

Turning the tables on fear

There's a Nightmare in My Closet, written and illustrated by Mercer Mayer, is a must for all preschoolers. Most young children are afraid of the dark at one time or another. To be able to talk about it and to find out that other children are afraid too is the start of working out the fear. We love to act out this story. It has only three characters—the boy and the two nightmares—but imagine being able to turn the tables on a childhood fear (a Nightmare in the closet) by *being* the fear. I always ask when we start—after I've picked the first three children — "Now are you *sure* you can look ugly enough to be the Nightmare?"

"Oh, yes, teacher—watch!"

The only prop you'll need is something a child can hide behind. Even a chair will do. When we act out this story, I read the story while the children "act," since there is little dialogue.

Caps for Sale, with both story and pictures by Esphyr Slobodkina, is the story of a peddler who sold caps; it is one of our favorites for acting out. You'll need six or seven inexpensive felt hats and a platform of some sort; we use the rocking boat, turned over.

The first day, read the story. Remember to explain, briefly, what a peddler is, and allow time for the children to talk about the story. On the second day, review the story and begin your acting. Pick a peddler, place the caps on his head. Encourage the peddler to walk up and down shouting, "Caps for sale! Caps for sale!"

The first time—sometimes every time—young children act out a story, they need encouragement. Quietly direct them: "The peddler is tired. He sits down by the tree (the rocking boat turned upside down). Everybody, sshhh!!!"

Quickly, while the peddler sleeps, pick as many children as the peddler has extra caps. Remember that he will need one for himself. Have the children climb onto the boat tree. Now direct the peddler to wake up and look to the right, then to the left—behind the tree—then up into the tree.

You must keep quietly telling the story, for in the excitement of acting it out, the children forget. Also, because all the children want a turn, you must keep up the pace: not fast, just a steady, storytelling pace. When the peddler starts his finger shaking and foot stomping and the monkeys imitate him, the children can hardly contain themselves.

Fat Cat, illustrated by Jack Kent, is a wonderful story for acting, with enough characters so you probably only have to do it twice to include all the children, and a story in which every character is important. Your preparation will be easy: a large piece of yellow-gold material (or a blanket) and a plastic bandage. One child is the Fat Cat, who is supposed to watch the porridge pot for the woman. He eats the pot and the porridge; then he eats her! As he travels through town, everyone asks what he's been eating to be so fat, and he eats them all!

As the Fat Cat eats the other characters, they climb under the blanket. When the woodcutter saves them by cutting open the cat, they all run out. You remember how much fun tents are, so you can imagine the giggling that goes on in that cat's tummy.

Anansi the Spider: A Tale from the Ashanti by Gerald McDermott has enough characters in all to make it possible for everyone to have a turn in three rounds of acting out. Each character in the story is important. Anansi the spider sets out on a journey. His life is threatened by a fish and a falcon, but he is saved by each of his six sons.

I hope acting out stories will be as much a joy for you as it's always been for me. Remember to be flexible and gentle—especially with the child who wants to participate but who gets halfway through and says, "Teacher, *you* say the words." Of course, you will. And if a child decides, in the middle of the act, to quit, everyone will clap and cheer for that child and let someone else finish. I can almost guarantee that by January you will have a preschool full of enthusiastic actresses and actors.

Letting children discover

games

As is the case with all the materials and activities presented in this book, I want to stress the importance of letting children discover. Sometimes we try to mask very serious learning by presenting it as a game, perhaps in the hope that we won't look as rigid, as structured if we do this. I think this kind of "pretending" is very harmful—perhaps even more harmful to our program than to the children, because it disguises the real learning that may be taking place, and we continue to delude ourselves that learning is something we *do to the child* rather than something that comes from *within the child*.

Just as I have certain criteria for judging music and stories, so I have certain criteria for judging whether games and other cooperative activities are usable with small children. Sometimes games and activities need to be modified for use with young children. Even though some of our fondest memories of childhood are the games we used to play, we forget that the memories probably stem from games we played in school when we were older than preschool age. Games can be fun for very young children, but there are special considerations for them. Games should be played for the joy of it. They are for fun!

Some young children, unfortunately, may have already played games in situations where the game was only for the skilled; if children haven't yet had this experience, they will be energetic, enthusiastic participants. If they have, you'll need to expose them to less demanding "gamesmanship" for a while before they'll want to get involved.

Remember, as with art, music, and all the questions that you may ask during circle, there isn't any right or wrong involved—you're not playing to teach specifics; you're playing so they will learn ten thousand things.

Second, games must be instant. Consider the attention span of young children when playing. Suppose you decide to play "Farmer in the Dell." There are eight characters, and the first character, the farmer, waits only ten or fifteen seconds to be chosen. But the poor cheese may have to wait five or six minutes! There are several ways to solve this problem: have two farmers, two wives, and thus more children to be chosen. Another way is to have two or three circles.

Third, keep it simple. Often even the simplest games have rules that are too difficult for young children to remember in the excitement of playing. We love "Duck, Duck, Goose" at our school, but in their enthusiasm, the children will often forget to run in opposite directions to arrive at the empty chair. I stand near the participating children and gently guide them in the right direction.

Fourth, no moving circles. Unless the circle is quite small, don't walk around holding hands. Often the youngest child (and sometimes an older child as well) falls, creating chaos. We all have a lifetime of chances to go around in circles. At this age, it's better to stand still in a circle and clap to the rhythm of the song. Sometimes, during free time, three or four children and I will make a circle and play a game in which we go around, but when even nine or ten children are involved, it's much more pleasant to stand still.

On moving in circles

policeman, policeman

We start playing "Policeman" in September, and whenever we have a few extra minutes, the children always say, "Please, teacher, let's play 'Policeman.'" It's a happy way to develop an awareness of other children and an easy way to introduce concepts of plaids, stripes, colors, polka-dots.

During circle, children can sit in chairs or on the floor. Do encourage children not to move around since the policeman must look at each child.

Pick a child to be policeman. It is important to guide the child gently to the center of the circle. Kneeling—so you have eye contact—in front of the child,

say, "I have lost my child. Do you think you can be a policeman and find him?" Of course they always can. Sometimes I add other questions. "Have you ever been a policeman? How long?"

They love it. Sometimes they'll respond, "Oh, yes. I've been a policeman for twenty years."

As you're talking, glance at another child and notice what that child is wearing. Now describe the other child. "My child has blond hair." Be sure to quickly explain "blond"—using another child as an example is fine. "He has brown eyes. He's wearing a blue shirt and brown and white plaid"—explain plaids—"pants, and he's been lost for three days, and I know he's hungry."

I am always amazed that most of our children can quickly find the "lost" child. Sometimes after I describe the "lost child" I get a little dramatic and weep a little about the "lost child." Often the "policeman" will console me and say, "Don't worry, teacher. I'll find him."

If the child is having a difficult time, ask, "Would you like me to tell you something else about my child? Well, he's a good friend of Robert's. And he likes to ride the big bike."

who is it?

Many times, when I hear a child shout outside or I overhear conversations between children, I cannot tell who it is without looking, but after we've played "Who Is It?" a few times, even my youngest preschoolers can tell instantly who's saying hello.

You'll need a soft bandana to use as a blindfold. During circle, or with four or five children gathered together, choose a child to be "it." Blindfold Mary, for example, explaining first that you're going to blindfold her so she can't see and that another child is going to stand in front of her and say, "Hello, Mary," and you want Mary to tell you who is talking.

If Mary can't tell who it is after a few seconds, help her out. Tell her something about the child. Encourage the other waiting children to be very quiet so that the blindfolded child can hear.

A variation is to proceed as above but have the blindfolded child touch the other child's hair, eyes, mouth, body, and tell you who it is. I even suggest that they smell each other, explaining that we all use different soaps and sometimes we smell different. Again, don't let the blindfolded child get confused. Help Mary with a few hints if she doesn't guess, but you'll be amazed at how perceptive children can become after they've played this a few times.

blind walk

Be sure to explain this "walk" first. Blindfold a child—keep him close to you and walk slowly about the school, stopping often to touch, smell, hug things. It's fun to do this outside, too—touch a tree, hug it—which tree is it? Young children will sometimes peek during blindfold games. It is a game, so don't exert pressure on them not to peek. Give them time and they'll feel secure enough to keep the blindfold on!

nose to nose

Each child needs a partner and stands facing him. Caller instructs children:

> Nose to nose
>
> Back to back
>
> Elbow to elbow.

Of course it's endless. Adults often misinterpret the instructions and keep the nose-to-nose position and try to get elbow-to-elbow at the same time. Children can also be the callers. They can do the calling while standing with a partner, or they can choose to stand in front of the group.

On changing partners

When I was first taught this game, the final step was to change partners; with very young children I don't do this. They've picked their partners for good reasons. They're secure with them, they love them, and changing partners often causes chaos and tears. And it takes too long. Often games are only played five to six minutes.

wolf

First, establish which children would like to clap and cheer. If you tell them which game it is, nobody will want to clap and cheer because everyone, including all the adults involved in the school, will want to play. Assure them they'll all have a turn to play. Next, choose a child to be the wolf. Everyone wants to be the wolf. Do it quickly to avoid the clamoring. You'll have to pick a safety area or zone to which the group can run when the wolf starts chasing them.

> The children ask the wolf: "Wolf, are you ready?"
>
> **Wolf:**   "No, I have to comb my hair."
>
> **Children:**   "Wolf, are you ready?"
>
> **Wolf:**   "No, I have to *(whatever he pleases)*."

When the wolf is finally ready, he (she) chases the children. If he catches one, that child becomes the wolf.

In playing "Wolf, Wolf" with young children you may run into a number of problems. For example, you will need to encourage them to try to fool each other rather than to repeat what you have said in demonstrating the game for them. Sometimes they won't run because they want to be caught in order to become the wolf. Sometimes the children who are wolves won't want to catch anyone because they love being the wolves so much.

The solution is to realize that there is no problem. Remember, this is a game! Be very relaxed about how you play it. If someone has had two wolf turns, tell that child to pick the new wolf. Voice inflection is important. Don't ask—just say, casually but firmly, "Tom, pick the new wolf. Quickly, so we'll all have a turn."

This summer we played "Wolf" with three- to eight-year-olds. They never tired of the game; they would ask at nine in the morning whether it was time to play "Wolf." On one occasion my assistant and I were busy with an art project and half-a-dozen children were organizing their own play. I observed them playing "Wolf." Sometimes they had two wolves and on one round went up to three. They later decided that three wolves for six players were too many!

It's interesting to me that the children love to run from the wolf and be caught, but that often they choose not be be chased in "Duck, Duck, Goose." Perhaps because "Wolf" involves ten or twelve other children being chased it is less anxiety producing than a one-to-one chase.

You will find children developing very creative answers to the "Wolf, are you ready?" questions. Sometimes they can be very graphic as well; one child this summer said, "No, I'm not ready! I have to sharpen my teeth!"

cat and mouse

We play a wonderful version of Cat and Mouse that our children love! You'll need two balls, one bigger than the other. Nerf® balls are great because they're so soft. We've used hard plastic balls very successfully also.

Start by telling a short story about how the Cat always chases the Mouse and the Mouse is little but quick. You can give them names if the children want to. The children are seated in a circle. The balls are handed from one child to another as quickly as possible. Start the small ball first and the large one a few seconds later. The object is, of course, for the big ball (Cat) to catch the little ball (Mouse). Of course the balls are dropped, and sometimes in all the excitement the Mouse or Cat is thrown. I stand or kneel in the circle to catch wayward balls.

In observing my children playing this game I think one of the reasons they are so enthusiastic is that most of them know what it's like to chase and to be chased. Sometimes we reverse the balls and go in the other direction—just for fun! You should hear the children cheering the Mouse and Cat on.

duck, duck, goose

At least once a week in our school, someone demands to play "Duck, Duck, Goose." It comes close, in my experience, to being the favorite game for three- to five-year-olds, even though they have a very hard time with the direction of the chase.

The children sit in a circle. One child walks around the outside of the circle, touching each head, saying "Duck" each time and then, after four or five taps, "Goose!" The child then runs around the circle away from the Goose, who is now chasing him, trying to get back to the empty place and sit down before being caught. If he makes it, the child who was named Goose becomes the new tapper.

Remember how long it takes young children to know "rules." Very often in the excitement of this game, the young child will run the wrong way around the circle. If you like, you can turn the child as soon as he jumps up, making sure he's facing the right way, but if he is already in motion, forget it. Just clap and cheer for him!

charades

We play a version of Charades in our school that can be as delightful for three-year-olds as for four- and five-year-olds. And everyone is involved. Before you play you will have to write some activities on cards. Pick a child to be "it" and whisper the activity you want him to demonstrate. Whoever guesses what he's doing can be the next to act out a new activity. Remember they can be very simple, two- to three-step activities. Consider what you know about the child.

Watching something scary on T.V.

Watching cartoons on T.V.

Getting on your trike and riding.

Getting off your trike.

Opening a birthday present.

Licking an ice cream cone; when some gets on your chin, licking it off.

Catching a ball.

Catching a ball and throwing it back.

Stubbing your toe getting dressed for school.

You can see that the activities are endless, but be prepared by having a sizable stack of suggestions. Sometimes a child will say: "I don't want to do that," or "That's too hard"—so be prepared to offer three or four other suggestions.

log roll

Four or five children are chosen to lie side-by-side, face down, with their arms tight by their sides or stretched over their heads. The child on the end rolls over the other children, then the second child starts. As they finish their roll they lie down quickly in position so the next roller can roll. The children love it. You can, of course, increase the number of children being logs, but we start small because the waiting is hard for the last child if you have ten rollers—and space is a consideration!

beach ball play

Beach balls are big, lightweight, harmless playthings for young children. Just tossing them back and forth is fun. Sometimes we have the children hold a ball between their stomachs and walk without touching the ball with their hands. They can also hold it between their heads. Unless you have lots of balls, consider this a game to play during free time. Very few young children want to sit around and watch four children play with a beach ball during circle.

the fifth test: gales of laughter

I sometimes get a sense that parents and teachers would be very happy to have a checklist of a thousand and one tasks to be given to each young child and checked off as they are accomplished as a demonstration that we have done everything we can to make the child perfect. No checklist in the world will make a child a good learner—a lover of learning, an eager discoverer, a person who wants to know!

It is in this spirit that I offer the materials of this chapter: materials that may not pass any other test in my school except that they are fun for both me and the children, materials that may not fit at all into my lesson plan, but which are exciting or pertinent to the particular day or simply spontaneous.

Valuing spontaneity

music

The value of music for young children cannot be overemphasized—for language development, musical development, fine and gross motor development —but most of all, for the sheer joy of it! Teachers need to orient all parents to these values; parents need to encourage their children's teachers to provide music if they're not already doing so. Parents need to orient each other, helping others to know how important music can be in providing an environment for communication with children.

If parents are music lovers and sing or play records frequently, their children will often bounce and move to musical stimuli when they are as young as nine or ten months. Children will, if they've been sung to by their parents, try music sounds like "Ba, ba, ba," or "La, la, la" before they speak. For the young child, music must be simple, like any activity involving young children. We must be careful not to impose adult standards; children often simply enjoy listening to an adult sing or hum.

In this time of wonderful technology, almost everyone has a record player. Many young children have ones of their own, and I see a tendency in parents and teachers to use records instead of singing to and with children themselves.

Perhaps it is that they feel inadequate compared to professional performers, but that round black disc or cassette tape does not hug, kiss, change words, or make up new verses. We have excellent records for children available today, and I recommend some of my favorites in Chapter 7, but we mustn't neglect the personal, the social, the familial sides of music.

One of the statements many parents and teachers make when I sing a new song or talk about the value of singing is, "But I can't sing—and I don't read music." It is, of course, helpful to be able to read music, nice if you have a piano to pick out a new tune. But music is for everyone. There are many ways to enjoy and appreciate music. One way to get started is to have a friend sing you a song six or seven times. If I'm trying to learn a song, I have someone sing it to me. And then I sing it, for everyone—my husband, my kids, my friends. Don't worry about whether you've changed the melody or gotten all the words right. Nobody will give you a gold star for doing this *perfectly*; you get a gold star for *singing*, period!

I would also hope to be able to inspire you to be unafraid to make up a song. We become locked into a fear of looking silly. Consider the light in a child's eyes before you decide not to take the risk. I would hope to inspire parents, grandparents, and friends of young children to share music from their own

No better gift

childhoods as well as new songs with children. There is no better gift you can give a child than an individual tradition.

Often when I do music workshops and stress that we must pass songs on from generation to generation, some parents' and teachers' immediate reaction is guilt. "I haven't done this"; "I don't remember any songs from my childhood." Don't look back. Start now developing some traditions.

music all day long

Music can and should be combined with other activities. When we fingerpaint with shaving cream at our school, we often put the record player near the fingerpainting area. It is wonderful to see three-, four-, and five-year-olds moving to music. Some of them can hardly contain themselves. We use all kinds of music—classical, sometimes quiet waltzes, sonatas, and sometimes wonderfully vibrant music like the Beethoven symphonies—and sometimes we use Dixieland, jazz, or bluegrass. We also place the record player near the fingerpainting when we do tabletop fingerpainting.

Sometimes we place the record player near the easel—but not so near that children drip paint on it. I've seen children move to the music and paint at the same time. We don't do this all the time. Children often socialize while painting, and if there were always music near the easels, we might be discouraging social interaction. It is important to vary the music here as well. We use nursery rhyme songs, classical marches, jazz, softly sung love songs.

Musical drawing is a wonderful rainy-day activity. It uses lots of energy. And the byproducts are small and large muscle development, eye-hand coordination, rhythm, and lots of movement.

Musical drawings should be done as often as possible—at least once or twice a week. Place large sheets of paper—one for each child—or roll out a long, wide piece of paper, let each child find a place, and give each child two or three crayons. I like paper at least thirty-six inches wide so children have plenty of personal space for big movement.

Tell the children to listen to the music and draw to it. Stop the music after a minute or so of playing and have them trade crayons if they want to, or have them use two crayons at once. Suggest they close their eyes and draw, feeling the music as they go; you'll love the way some of them "squint."

What kind of music? We start with classical. I prefer a record with many different selections so that I can change the music every thirty to forty seconds and have the children change crayons.

The musical selections are only as limited as you wish to make them. Once you get started on musical drawings, you'll be trying all sorts of wonderful possibilities. Some suggestions to get you started:

> **Strauss:** Josef and Johann Strauss wrote wonderful waltzes, polkas, and *galops.* Try to find a recording with a good variety.
>
> **Rossini:** The children love the "Overture" to *William Tell.*
>
> **Chopin:** We use *Sonata No. 2 in B-Flat Minor* often. It starts slowly; then the tempo quickens. His "Polonaise in A" is wonderful.
>
> **Ravel:** *Bolero.*
>
> **Tschaikovsky:** *Nutcracker Suite* is recognized by many children.
>
> **Bach, Beethoven, Brahms:** Be sure to include at least one recording of each. Beethoven's *Ninth Symphony* is especially marvelous for this activity. In starting your collection, you might want to begin with a single recording of the "Bach's Greatest," "Beethoven's Greatest" type. Often, the melodies will be familiar, and you can expand from this simple start.
>
> **Pops:** For sheer enjoyment, try the sound track from *The Sting.* The children will all think they're piano players! Try a jazz album; your local record store may be able to recommend something interesting. "Dueling Banjos" from *Deliverance* is wonderful for its upbeat rhythms, as is most banjo music.

Most important, try anything you play at least *twice.* Sometimes it will take a few sessions to loosen the children up. Sometimes a piece of music will be too long for young children. If the children seem restless, move it along—change records—do something more lively!

If we have a new record, I put it on during the free times, and as the children are painting, working with clay, or doing puzzles, they hear the record. I'm

always delighted, and rather amazed—even after fifteen years—when we start to sing the "new" song, to find that some of the children can already sing part of it.

singing

Sometimes when the children are fingerpainting, sometimes when they're swinging, sometimes when they're climbing, I sing to them, using a familiar tune. I sing—to the tune of "Jingle Bells," for example—

> **Fingerpaint, fingerpaint!**
> **Moving all around,**
> **Your hands go this way**
> **And that way;**
> **Your hands go all about!**

When they're swinging, I might sing something like this:

> **Gavin's in a swing, and the swing goes high;**
> **Leslie's in a swing, and the swing goes high.**
> **Swinging,**
> **Swinging,**
> **Bye and bye.**

Obviously, the song does not have to rhyme. Remember my caution not to worry about sounding silly.

I often sing a song about three kids in a swing (we have a tire swing that holds three), and I repeat the line often: "Three kids in a swing, and the swing goes high." Then I sing or chant something like:

> **Mikey's in the swing, and he's wearing blue pants,**
> **Jake's in the swing, and he has blue eyes,**
> **Erica's in the swing, and she's wearing red socks,**
> **La, la, la, la, la.**

Because I am enthusiastic, and because they have a model, the children will sometimes make up verses. Keep it simple and spontaneous. You're not out for a recording contract. But I hope you can see from my examples how we can at the same time encourage children to observe and articulate their observations —what others are wearing, what color their eyes are, how old they are (see "Policeman, Policeman," Chapter 5).

One important rule I have for myself about singing when the children are playing is that I am very careful not to interfere with their play and never to interrupt interaction between children. I would never jump into the playhouse area where two or three children are playing house and start singing, "Erica's a mommy." That kind of play is more important at that moment than a song. When children are interacting, be quiet! Listen! Develop your sense of timing.

Music doesn't have to be a group activity. Music is spontaneous. You know how as adults we feel sometimes as if we could burst into song. Children feel like that, too. When a young child is singing, humming, or just moving to music, try simply to be there. Sometimes they'll ask you to sing with them. Enjoy that moment. Occasionally, a few more children will join in.

Often teachers of young children have a formal time set aside for music— 10:00 to 10:15 A.M., for example. What works better for me is to sing a couple of songs just before sharing; just before story time, we'll sing another song or two. For the young child, fifteen straight minutes of music might be too much. Then "music time" becomes frustrating for children and adults. We all have our own nominee for the person who can sing more songs in ten minutes than any other preschool teacher in the world. That's hardly the idea.

rags

Some songs, like "You Are My Sunshine," are kept alive from generation to generation on the sheer strength of everybody's knowing and loving them. Others resurface from time to time, and I, at least, always wonder how I could have forgotten to sing these songs to each new group of children. Last year, a teacher reminded me of "Rags." Children love it. Parents delight in the movements. A teacher told me this summer, a little tearfully, that when she first started teaching twenty-five years ago, she did a whole PTA program revolving around "Rags"!

I've got a dog and his name is Rags;
(Use hands for ears on each side of head)
He eats so much that his tummy sags!
(Both arms in front of tummy)
His ears flip-flop,
(Wag hands on each side of head)
And his tail wig-wags
(Wiggle bottom)
And when he walks, he walks zig-zag!
(Point left hand to right, right hand to left)

Chorus:
He goes flip-flop,
(Wag hands on each side of head)
Wig-wag,
(Wiggle bottom)
Zig-zag!
(Point left hand to right, right hand to left)
He goes flip-flop,
Wig-wag, { *Repeat motions* }
Zig-zag!
I love Rags, and he loves me!
(Hug yourself, rocking from side to side)

My dog Rags, he loves to play,
He rolls around in the mud all day.
(Roll arms)
I whistle,
(All whistle)
He doesn't obey!
(Shake head from side to side)
He always runs the other way!
(Point the other way)

rags

I've got a dog and his name is Rags; he eats so much that his tummy sags! His

ears flip-flop, and tail wig- wags, and when he walks, he walks zig-zag! He goes

flip-flop, wig-wag, zig-zag! He goes flip-flop, wig-wag, zig-zag! He goes

flip-flop, wig-wag, zig-zag! I love Rags, and he loves me!

turn the page, turn the page

A few years ago, a teacher taught me the words to this delightful song. I couldn't remember the melody she'd used, so I made up my own. Begin by asking the children to take out their music books. Demonstrate by pulling at your own back pocket and then holding your hands in front of you as if you were holding a book. As you sing, turn each page of your make-believe book.

Of all the songs we do, this one is the most fun. Children are such believers. They take out their books and turn the page so seriously at the end of each line. Sometimes a child will say, "Teacher Bev, I forgot my book."

I respond, "Look on with someone."

If I had the wings of an airplane
(Spoken: Turn the page, turn the page)
Up in the air I would fly.
(Spoken: Turn the page, turn the page)
There I would stay as an airplane
(Spoken: Turn the page, turn the page)
Until the day that I die.
(Spoken: Turn the page, turn the page)

Chorus: *(May be repeated. We often do it three or four times.)*
Ooh la, la, Ooh la, la, Ooh, la, la!
(Spoken: Turn the page, turn the page)
Ooh la, la, Ooh la, la, La!
(Spoken: Turn the page, turn the page)
Ooh la, la, Ooh la, la, Ooh, la, la!
(Spoken: Turn the page, turn the page)
Ooh la, la, Ooh la, la, la!
(Spoken: Now that's all for today. Close your books and put them away.)

While I love this song for children, it's even more fun with adults. When I say, "Take out your books," there's instant panic.

People whisper, look at each other questioningly—"What book? No one said anything about bringing a book!"

The song reminds adults of that panicky feeling children have very often when adults demand, "Where's your jacket?" "Where's your homework?" It's nice to be reminded what it's like to be a child.

turn the page, turn the page

If I had the wings of an airplane, up in the air I would fly.

There I would stay as an airplane, until the day that I die.

Ooh la, la, ooh la, la, ooh la, la! Ooh la, la, ooh la, la, la!

Ooh la, la, ooh la, la, ooh la, la! Ooh la, la, ooh la, la, la!

skinna-ma-rink

This song combines nonsense and affection. What more could you ask for young children? The sun and the moon? They're here in the movements!

Skinna-ma-rink-a-dink-a-dink,
    (Cup right elbow in left hand; semaphore with right hand and forearm)
Skinna-ma-rink-a-doo, *(Reverse above)*
I *(Point to eye)*
Love *(Cover heart with right hand; pat right hand with left)*
You! *(Point to someone)*

Skinna-ma-rink-a-dink-a-dink,
    (Cup right elbow in left hand; semaphore with right hand and forearm)
Skinna-ma-rink-a-doo, *(Reverse above)*
I *(Point to eye)*
Love *(Cover heart with right hand; pat right hand with left)*
You! *(Point to someone)*

I love you in the morning *(Make the sun by arching arms overhead)*
And in the afternoon; *(Bring arch to midpoint on body)*
I love you in the evening *(Bring arch down to knees)*
And underneath the moon. *(Rock the arch from side to side over your head)*

Skinna-ma-rink-a-dink-a-dink,
    (Repeat semaphore)
Skinna-ma-rink-a-doo, *(Reverse semaphore)*
I *(Point to eye)*
Love *(Cover heart with right hand; pat right hand with left)*
You! *(Point to someone)*

telling stories

Telling stories is a wonderful experience for both storyteller and listeners. There's a magic about sitting close to the children and watching them as you tell a story: there are no barriers—no book, no flannelboard. You can touch, hug, or hold a child's hand as you tell a story. You can move around if you like, stopping to sit close to a child you sense needs it.

skinna-ma-rink

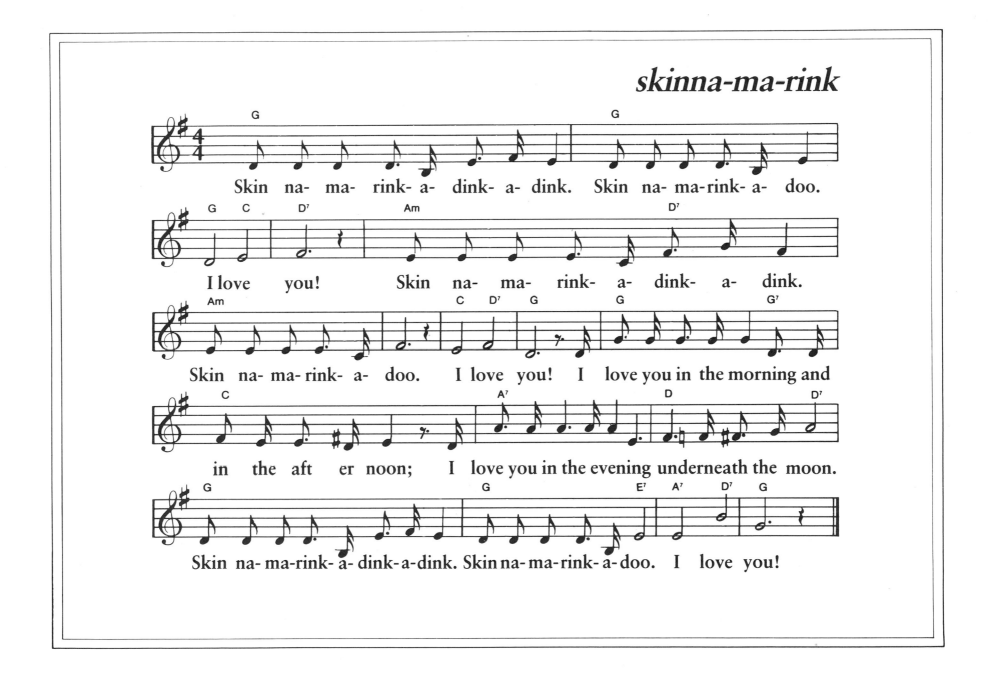

Imagining a rolling sea, a forest

It's important to know a story—even if you're reading it, but especially if you're telling it. Sometimes I am very dramatic when telling a story, sometimes very quiet. Sometimes I use lots of gestures to demonstrate what's happening. Telling a story encourages the children's creativity because without the visual aid of the book illustration, they are encouraged to imagine a storm, a rolling sea, a forest, a monster.

I never insist that children sit perfectly still during a storytelling. Sometimes they must jump up and demonstrate for me how it is. How do I handle this? I encourage them with a, "Yes, yes," and then I move on. They're always ready to hear the rest of the story.

Ideally, you should tell a story at least once a week. It doesn't have to be long. Sometimes, try telling a story without the book the day after you've read it. If a child asks to see the book, I will sometimes say, "I took it back to the library, but I think we can tell it without the book. You can help me."

Especially since television, children seem to be hearing fewer and fewer tales—folk tales or personal stories passed down from generation to generation. Everyone involved with children — parents, teachers, grandparents, baby-sitters, friends—needs to help revive the art of the folk story. Most of us know at least one story passed down from generation to generation. We must summon up the wonderful experiences of our own childhood and pass them along to our own children. There are also many books of tales available in the library; just ask your librarian. Don't be afraid to change an old tale a little—to shorten it or lengthen it. Your children will be enthralled.

Finally, don't take it for granted that all children know the old standards. When we started using nursery rhyme stickers to encourage the children to write their own stories, we discovered that many of them didn't know what we, anyway, would consider the tired old favorites.

Cindy and Zip

One five-year-old looked at a "Mary Had a Little Lamb" sticker and proceeded to tell a delightful story: "This little girl is walking her dog. The girl's name is Cindy. Her dog's name is Zip." We didn't interfere with the story, of course, since it belonged to her, but we no longer take the old standards for granted and spend considerable time telling and acting out nursery rhymes as well as favorite old stories and poems.

The child as curriculum

"special" projects

Although special days or weeks should be planned so that they incorporate many of the positive values of identity reinforcement, changing, creating, and cooperating, it's probably a mistake to approach these projects initially in anything but a spirit of pure enjoyment. I'll discuss five projects we do every year because the children have so much fun with them—Lollipop Day, Popcorn Week, Rainbow Week, Monster Week, and Pajama Day (which always turns out to be a week before it's over).

We do many more special days and projects than these, of course, and I'd also like to stress that we do not confine the activities of these days or weeks to the calendar in which they first appear. Many of the activities from these projects carry over into the regular year.

It's very important to respond to a child's need for a book, a story, a project when the child wants to do it or to repeat it—not to turn the child away by saying, "We'll do that later when we have Monster Week." Or, "We already did that during Pajama Day." Remember, at this age particularly, the child *is* the curriculum.

lollipop day

We stress good nutrition at our school, as do most schools, I'm sure, but one of the best days of our year is absolutely non-nutritious—at least from a physical standpoint; I'm not so sure it's not *very* nutritious on other levels.

In preparation for Lollipop Day, we make a simple construction paper tree, on which we draw lollipops with felt pens. We then tell the story of the lollipop tree—very simply and quickly. Once a child planted a lollipop stick, watering it well and hoping it would grow. One day the child awoke to find a tree all full of lollipops! He sat beneath the tree and looked up, and when he opened his mouth, a lollipop dropped right in!

You may wish to use the recording to reinforce the story. We use The Limelighters' *Through Children's Eyes;* it's well done, and there's a wonderful chorus that all our children and parents love to sing.

After you've told the story and listened to the recording, plant a lollipop stick, preferably beneath a tree in your play yard, and water it. Make sure everybody's hoping.

Very early the next morning, before the children arrive, staple or tape lollipops to the tree beneath which you planted the stick. If you don't have a tree, plant a branch in a sand-filled can. I would advise a few extra lollipops to give to visitors and to replace lollipops that get dropped in the dirt or sand. Let the children discover the lollipops for themselves. At three and four, they are such believers in magic, and this stage lasts for such a short time!

There are some traps accompanying Lollipop Day that you will want to try to circumvent: first, when the first child discovers the tree, be there! If you're not, in their enthusiasm one or two children will manage to get all the lollipops.

Second, beware the five-year-old skeptic. Last year, for the first time, a jaded five-year-old exclaimed, "Teacher, you stapled them on there, didn't you!" I explained to Josh very gently and quietly that I in fact I had, but that we should keep it a secret in order not to spoil the magic for Ross—a three-year-old whom Josh really cared about. The thought that he might spoil the magic for Ross made Josh keep the secret. I heard him later saying to another five-year-old, "Nobody puts them on! It's just magic!!"

Finally, you may have some children who will want to repeat the experiment at home. When it doesn't work, they're very disappointed. I tell my parents beforehand that they need to impress on their children that magic happens only in special places and that school is a special place.

popcorn week

Perhaps it's the smell, perhaps it's the noise or the sense of apprehension in waiting for each pop—maybe it's a combination of many good associations, but popcorn is a favorite topic in almost any school.

Start the week by sharing the unpopped kernels. Pass them around. Smell them. Talk about their smoothness, their color, their size.

Then place two large, old sheets on the floor. Have the children sit around the *outside* edge of the sheets. Encourage other teachers and parents to be involved; it's crucial that no child get burned. Place a popcorn popper in the middle of the sheet, and leave the lid off, allowing the popcorn to dance. In the excitement that follows, the children can easily forget to stay off the sheets, and you must be constantly aware of the group's movements. After I have removed the popper, the children eat the popcorn.

Now for the dance: encourage the children to make themselves as small as possible, remembering that there's no right or wrong way to be a popcorn kernel—they're all different.

Chant or sing a popcorn song. Always ask for the children's help when creating a song. The popcorn song changes every year in our school.

> Oh, oh, I'm very small.
> Curl up in a pot like a ball.
> First I'm yellow, soon I'll be white.
> I'm going to pop, pop, pop.

Space the chanting of "pop." Let it be an erratic rhythm. Expect the dance to be jerky and erratic and for arms and legs move in all directions. Some children won't pop. They've noticed that a few kernels are always left in the bottom of the pan.

Tomie De Paola's *The Popcorn Book* is the only book you'll need. It's a delightful, well-illustrated history of popcorn in America. The book was written for young children.

At least once during Popcorn Week we have popcorn. Do not add salt or butter. We add milk and a little sugar. The Pilgrims ate it as a breakfast cereal. The children always love it, and our parents moan and groan.

Later in the week, try writing a popcorn poem. Encourage each child to say one word about popcorn. The result will be a rhythmic collection of words that you can write out and hang up as part of the week's decoration.

Sometimes the children will make up words like "poppity" and "crunchery." Use these very descriptive words in your poem without changing them.

pop

jumpty yummy

white

butter

salty

After a couple of days of popping, write a story about popcorn. I ask each child to tell me something about popcorn. Be patient. Let the story flow from the children. Remember that anything they say is important. What about repetition? Laura says, "I like the popping sound." Michael says, "I like the popping, too." Write it as they say it. Encourage each child to say something different, but if they don't want to, write the story as they tell it.

Finally, there's a great popcorn song, with suggestions for movement, on Steve Millang and Greg Scalsa's *We All Live Together,* Volume 2.

rainbow week

"The World Is a Rainbow" is a beautifully written song from Steve Millang and Greg Scalsa's *We All Live Together.* We have almost made the song our school song for its important message—"It takes all kinds of people to make the world go around."

Children need very little encouragement to be fascinated by rainbows. Certainly there are rainbows everywhere these days—transparent rainbows to stick on windows, rainbow pins, rainbow candles, stuffed rainbows. At some specialty shops they even stock a special pair of plastic glasses that produces visions of rainbows when they're used to look at lights. Some urban areas have full-scale rainbow shops: and we haven't even mentioned prisms and crystals!

Explain to the children, as simply as possible, what makes a rainbow—the reflection of the sun's ray on rain or mist. Then just enjoy making rainbows, dancing rainbow dances, writing rainbow verses and songs, telling rainbow stories, reading rainbow books!

Last year, to kick off Rainbow Week, we made a huge construction paper rainbow by stapling arc-cut paper together; on one side of the rainbow, we attached a cloud. The children also enjoy placing smaller colored arcs cut from construction paper on a flannelboard.

Have available a selection of inexpensive scarves in all colors and encourage "rainbow dancing" to music that encourages light, cloud-like movement; or dance to "The World Is a Rainbow."

There are excellent rainbow books available for this activity: Don Freeman's *A Rainbow of My Own* is especially nice for the young child. Ul DeRico's *The Rainbow Goblins* is the magnificently illustrated story of the rainbow goblins that lived on color. A book to look at and be shown in small groups is *Rainbows* by Thom Klika.

Rainbow rhymes are easy; you might have to start the children out with a first line:

"Rainbows are beautiful.

I love the blue.

What rhymes with blue?"

Keep it going until everyone that wants to has had a chance to participate.

Have each child contribute a line or two to write a rainbow story. Encourage them gently to tell you how they feel about rainbows: would they like to climb a rainbow? What color do they like best? Sometimes making a statement about your own feelings encourages them and they'll expand.

I've said, "I'd like a rainbow on my bedroom wall."

A child responded, "Oh, teacher, I want one on my ceiling so when I go to bed I can see the rainbow watching me!"

monster week

Talking about fears

Like nightmares in the closet and dragons under the bed, children create monsters. Monster Week provides a positive way for young children to talk about their fears in the form of monsters.

We start the week by making a huge monster, seven feet tall—just a rather abstract figure. We make it double, stapling it together and stuffing it with newspaper to give it dimension. Then everyone helps decorate it with felt pens, cotton balls, crayons, paint, yarn, styrofoam pieces, sticky dots, and anything else that comes to hand.

We always discuss at length the name we want to give our large monster.

We also serve monster food, and our parents really put a great deal of effort into creating it: green mashed potatoes; cheese, tinted gruesome colors, to spread on crackers; extras like shredded carrots, thawed frozen peas to make ugly faces. Sometimes the children have ideas about what monsters eat also.

Each child also makes an individual, smaller version of the large monster. They all give their monsters names and often write stories about them. We read the stories during sharing or circle time. This is a story our children produced as a joint effort last year.

A Monster Story

Once upon a time I had a monster. He was ten feet long. He had two legs and he had six arms. He had one head. He had four eyeballs. He had a hundred hairs—they were purple. He had a hundred extra legs—seven legs all around. He had a hundred noses. He had 268 spiders on his head. He has a lot of stomach. I'm going to chop his head off. He had a hundred mouths. He had a birthday—he's four. He has a thousand feet and one-hundred ears. He has a pony tail. He has a banana up his nose. He grew to a hundred feet. Sixty cheeks. He was bald. He's purple and red striped. He lives in the forest.

pajama day

A few years ago, a parent at our school suggested that having a Pajama Day might be fun. It's more than fun! Pajama Day presents a wonderful opportunity for children to talk about sleeping habits, dreams, nightmares, and a whole realm of important experiences. There's no doubt in my mind that from the viewpoint of productive activities for the child, Pajama Day is one of the best projects we do.

Send a note home telling parents that Pajama Day is coming up. Talk about Pajama Day in advance to the children; don't under any circumstances make wearing pajamas mandatory. Stress the fun. "Yes, you can wear your bathrobe." Discuss what would be nice to have for snack on Pajama Day.

On the day itself, teachers and participating parents should also wear their pajamas and bathrobes. (I'm always concerned about emergencies, so I fudge a little and wear clothes under my bathrobe.)

Prepare art materials — light and dark papers, crayons and felt pens, and suggest that children do a nighttime picture. Have felt pens and paper at the writing table and encourage the children to tell a nighttime story or a story about bedtime or sleeping.

For sharing, you can assemble a hot water bottle, a pillow, a blanket (one with satin binding if possible), a brick or a large stone, and a towel to wrap the brick in. I warm the brick, wrap it in a towel and put warm water in the hot water bottle, and we talk about how some people keep warm at night. Many of our children have never seen a hot water bottle. The children talk about heating pads and electric blankets too.

I lay the pillow on the floor and get the blanket ready, and we "share" how we sleep. The reason I suggested the satin binding on the blanket is that many children like to feel satin. Each child is encouraged to demonstrate, and many of the children comment on other modes of sleeping, such as, "My brother does that too!" The process of letting each child show how he sleeps can seem overwhelming, but while being careful not to rush each child, you *can* move it along!

For snack, we usually have something wonderful like pancakes. With two large griddles and plenty of batter and help, the children ladle a scoop of pancake batter and make their own pancakes. Other suggestions for snack: muffins (which the children can make themselves); English muffins and scrambled eggs—they love to crack eggs (what are a few shells?); even oatmeal is fun if everyone agrees.

There are some wonderful night stories for circle time. You need to make use of your library and certainly you will find some that I don't mention. *There's a Nightmare in My Closet* by Mercer Mayer provides a wonderful opportunity to talk about nightmares. Allow ample time for each child to talk about his or her nightmares. When they start sharing, ask, "Shall we write these down?" Have a list of all the children's names, so one or two words beside each name is enough for discussion later.

Another good book is *It's Time to Go to Bed* by Joyce Segal, illustrated by Robin Eaton. This is a delightful book to illustrate the many excuses children use when their moms say, "Time to go to bed!"

"When a mother goldfish says it's time to go to bed, the little goldfish dive straight down to the bottom of the goldfish bowl. They never say, 'I want a drink of water.'"

Bed Book by Sylvia Plath is a wonderful book with many delightful imaginary beds. All the children shout and argue about their favorite.

Hush Little Baby. A Folk Lullabye, illustrated by Aliki, is another treasure.

Mothers, fathers, grandparents have sung this song to children for years. Its familiarity is soothing and comforting for children. This book is a must.

One wonderful talk we had during the "week" of Pajama Day started like this: I said, "The last thing I do before I go to sleep is . . . ." And each child shared:

"Shut the closet door."

"Kiss the dog."

"Brush my teeth."

"Hug my mom."

"Look under the bed for monsters."

Finding out that other children and the teacher look under the bed too is *such* a relief to young children. Don't you remember as a young child feeling absolutely alone because of certain fears and feeling silent relief when someone else mentioned the same fear? The opportunity to talk about fears helps them disappear.

Music and movement for Pajama Day can be varied. Don't forget "Five Little Monkeys" (see Chapter Three). For goodness' sakes, sing "Rock-a-Bye Baby." The children love it; they laugh and generally ham it up. "Wee Willie Winkie" is another favorite; don't forget the bell or triangle at the end.

> Wee Willie Winkie runs through the town
> Upstairs and downstairs in his nightgown,
> Rapping at the window, crying through the lock,
> "Are the children in their beds, for now it's eight o'clock!"

"Little Boy Blue" goes to sleep, too, and remember

Bye Baby Bunting,
Daddy's gone a-hunting,
Gone to get a rabbit skin
To wrap his baby bunting in.

Lullaby is not a familiar word to many young children. Talk about lullabies. Sing some. Have the children help write a new lullaby. If you can't sing a lullaby, chant it softly.

Writing a new lullaby doesn't have to be complicated. Simplicity is the key when writing music with children. One year my children made up this song to the tune of Brahms's "Lullaby," which we had been humming.

Go to sleep, go to sleep,
Don't jump on the bed.
If you do, if you do,
You'll fall on your head!

Finally, you mustn't forget to play "Ten in a Bed."

Ten in bed, and the little one said, "Roll over, roll over"
Well, they all rolled over and one fell out.
Nine in a bed, and the little one said, "Roll over, roll over"
Well, they all rolled over, and one fell out.

After all nine children have fallen out, the last child says, "Alone at last!"

It should be apparent that Pajama Day is both simple and highly complex. Since all the children must have sufficient time to talk, draw, write, and sing about sleep, nightmares, dreams, and bedtime, Pajama Day always extends into a second day for us, and sometimes three days are necessary.

I hope I have been able to show how Pajama Day opens the door for many different stories, songs, fingerplays, dramatic play, and most of all how it presents young children with the opportunity to talk about a time of day that sometimes troubles or scares them and is therefore a time when parents need to be especially sensitive to the needs of each child.

resources

No matter what I've included on my plan for the day—and it would be very difficult to teach without an overall plan—if I find a new book or hear about a new record or game, then the new book, record, or game takes precedence over the plan. People who not only remain open to new materials, but actively seek them out remain interested in life and interesting to children. These teachers will be better able to foster learning in their students because enthusiasm about learning is attractive.

choosing books

There's something quite wonderful about the way teachers share materials: some of the passing on of authors, stories, songs is almost akin to folklore. But informal sharing of books, as marvelous as it is, isn't enough. A regular pattern of visits to a good bookstore and visits to a good children's department in a local library is necessary to keep a teacher's list of book resources up to date.

The same should hold true for parents, who should not confine their attention to books to spur-of-the-moment buying at the supermarket. When I observe parents buying books for their young children in the grocery store, I want to grab the intercom and shout, "Please, Moms and Dads, do you have any idea how many wonderful books there are in the library?" One of the most wonderful gifts parents can give their children is "the library habit."

Children do need to have books of their own, of course, but most of the ones I'd recommend couldn't be purchased at the local supermarket. When I am looking for books to read to my children at school or for books for my grandchildren, I browse, but I always keep an eye open for books by my favorite authors. These writers are my favorites because their stories are always written for the joy of reading and with a strong sense of what children like. Just as important for this age group, the illustrations are charming and especially appealing to children.

I am always on the lookout for new material from the following writers, for example, because I have had such tremendous success using their work with my children: Jose Aruego, Eric Carle, Tomie DePaola, Mirra Ginsburg, Leo Lionni, Mercer Mayer, Maurice Sendak, William Steig, and Harve Zemach. I would think most preschool teachers would agree on the reliability of most or all of these authors.

You must, of course, even with your most trusted authors, read the book in advance to make certain that it is appropriate for the age group you are presenting it to. Sometimes, as with some of Mirra Ginsburg's stories, if you "read" from the book, it may be too wordy for three- to four-year-olds. Many times you can shorten—by not reading every word—and still have a delightful story for very young children. Be aware, too, that if you're reading to only two or three children who have an appropriate attention span, you can sometimes read every word of a very involved book.

a list of favorites

I heartily recommend any of the books on the following list for use with young children—either directly or as resource material. Some of them, unfortunately,

A wonderful African tale.

Not heavy-handed.

Used on our reading platform.

Has to be done three or four times. Beware of overexplaining. Let the children find African animals in their environment.

are out of print as of the date of this writing; I would suggest that they are well worth looking for in libraries or used book stores. I hope all these books will become favorites of yours, if you are not using them already, but the broader purpose of the list, like the purpose of this book, is to inspire you to develop and share your *ongoing* list of favorite books for young children. Selections marked "No Words" are especially good for eliciting a response from young children.

Aardema, Verna. *Why Mosquitoes Buzz in People's Ears.* New York: The Dial Press, 1975.

Alderson, Brian. *Cakes and Custards.* New York: William Morrow and Co., 1975.

Alexander, Martha. *Blackboard Bear.* New York: The Dial Press, 1977.

———. *Nobody Asked Me if I Wanted a Baby Sister.* New York: The Dial Press, 1977.

———. *No Ducks in our Bathtub.* New York: The Dial Press, 1977.

Adoff, Arnold. *Make a Circle. Keep Us In: Poems for a Good Day.* New York: Delacorte Press, 1975.

Aliki, illus. *Hush Little Baby: A Folk Lullabye.* Englewood Cliffs, New Jersey: Prentice-Hall, Inc., 1968.

Anno, Mitsumasa. *Anno's Alphabet.* New York: Harper & Row Publishers, Inc., 1975.

———. *Anno's Counting Book.* New York: Harper & Row Publishers, Inc., 1977.

———. *Anno's Journey.* New York: Philomel Books, 1980.

Aruego, Jose. *A Crocodile's Tale.* New York: Scholastic Book Service, 1976.

Aruego, Jose and Ariane. *Look What I Can Do.* New York: Charles Scribner's Sons, 1971.

———. *We Hide, You Seek.* New York: Greenwillow Books, 1979.

Barton, Byron. *Buzz, Buzz, Buzz*. New York: Macmillan Publishing Co., Inc., 1973.

A perennial favorite for acting out.

Blair, Susan, illus. *The Three Billy Goats Gruff: A Norwegian Folk Tale*. New York: Scholastic Book Service, 1970.

Brand, Oscar. *When I First Came to This Land*. New York: G. P. Putnam's Sons, 1974.

Brown, Ruth. *A Dark, Dark Tale*. New York: The Dial Press, 1981.

Beautifully illustrated. One of those books children demand again and again. I purchased this in March and read it right away; we've read it every month since, and it will still be great for Halloween. On each page, the children can find hidden birds, animals.

Brown, Margaret Wise. *A Child's Good Night Book*. Reading, Massachusetts: Addison-Wesley Publishing Co., Inc., 1943.

———. *The Golden Egg Book*. Golden Books, 1947.

———. *Goodnight Moon*. New York: Harper & Row Publishers, Inc., 1977.

Pajama Day.

———. *Runaway Bunny*. New York: Harper & Row Publishers, Inc., 1977.

Great for Easter.

Burningham, John. *Would You Rather . . .* New York: Harper & Row Publishers, Inc., 1978.

Nonsense; especially good for getting responses from children.

Calhoun, Mary. *The Sweet Patootie Doll*. New York: William Morrow and Co., 1957.

Make a sweet potato (or yam) doll and let the children hold it.

Carle, Eric. *The Grouchy Ladybug*. New York: Harper & Row Publishers, Inc., 1977.

———. *Have You Seen My Cat?* New York: Franklin Watts, 1973.

———. *I See a Song*. New York: Harper & Row Publishers, Inc., 1973.

———. *Pancakes, Pancakes*. New York: Alfred A. Knopf, Inc., 1970.

———. *The Secret Birthday Message*. New York: Harper & Row Publishers, Inc., 1972.

———. *The Very Hungry Caterpillar*. New York: Philomel Books, 1970.

Carr, Rachel. *Be a Frog, a Bird, or a Tree.* New York: Harper & Row Publishers, Inc., 1977.

DeAngeli, Marguerite. *Book of Nursery and Mother Goose Rhymes.* New York: Doubleday & Co., Inc., 1954.

DePaola, Tomie. *Charlie Needs a Cloak.* New York: Scholastic Book Service, 1973.

————. *The Cloud Book.* New York: Holiday House, 1975.

————. *The Knight and the Dragon.* New York: G. P. Putnam's Sons, 1980.

————. *Pancakes for Breakfast.* New York: Harcourt, Brace, Jovanovich, Inc., 1978.

————. *The Popcorn Book.* New York: Scholastic Book Service, 1979.

————. *Strega Nona.* Englewood Cliffs, New Jersey: Prentice-Hall, Inc., 1975.

DeRegnier, Beatrice. *Catch a Little Fox.* New York: Houghton Mifflin Co., 1978.

————. *Willy O'Dwyer Jumped in the Fire.* New York: Atheneum Publishers, 1968.

de Rico, Ul. *The Rainbow Goblins.* New York: Thames Hudson, 1978.

Dodson, Fitzhugh. *I Wish I had a Computer that Makes Waffles.* La Jolla, California: Oaktree Publications, Inc., 1978.

Domanska, Janina. *The Turnip.* New York: Macmillan Publishing Co., Inc., 1969.

Duff, Maggie. *Rum, Pum, Pum: A Folk Tale.* New York: Macmillan Publishing Co., Inc., 1978.

Edens, Cooper. *The Caretakers of Wonder.* La Jolla, California: Green Tiger Press, 1980.

————. *If You're Afraid of the Dark: Remember the Night Rainbow.* La Jolla, California: Green Tiger Press, 1981.

Nice to have as suggestions for movement.

An especially good collection.

I would first read this with less detail than is here. The next time, I would read a little more.

Great for Pajama Day. Ask the children what task they'd like to perform. My favorite response remains Erica's, who said she thought the weatherman did all that.

Not many words. Good for Pajama Day.

Good to act out in a group; use on a windy day.

Action stuff.

We use jump-rope rhymes for movement and transition. Perhaps children's short attention spans account for their delight in short, simple rhyming chants; perhaps they also take great pride in being able to remember and repeat an entire short chant. This book is a wonderful reference!

Especially good for the "What's going to happen now?" technique.

If you go slowly enough, the children will guess who his grandpa and grandma are.

Ets, Marie Hall. *Gilberto and the Wind.* New York: The Viking Press, 1963.

Flack, Marjorie and Kurt Wiese. *The Story about Ping.* New York: Penguin Books, 1977.

Fowke, Edith. *Ring Around the Moon.* Englewood Cliffs, New Jersey: Prentice-Hall Inc., 1977.

———. *Sally Go Round the Sun.* New York: Doubleday & Co., Inc., 1970.

Freeman, Don. *Beady Bear.* New York: The Viking Press, 1954.

———. *A Rainbow of My Own.* New York: Penguin Books, 1978.

Frost, Robert L. *Stopping by Woods on a Snowy Evening.* New York: E. P. Dutton, 1978.

———. *You Come Too. Favorite Poems for Young Readers.* New York: Holt, Rinehart & Winston, 1959.

Galdone, Paul, illus. *The Hare and the Tortoise.* New York: McGraw-Hill Book Co., 1962.

Ginsburg, Mirra. *The Chick and the Duckling.* New York: Macmillan Publishing Co., Inc., 1972.

———. *How the Sun Was Brought Back to the Sky.* New York: Macmillan Publishing Co., Inc., 1975.

———. *Mushroom in the Rain.* New York: Macmillan Publishing Co., Inc., 1978.

———. *The Strongest One of All.* New York: Greenwillow Books, 1977.

———. *Where Does the Sun Go at Night?* New York: Greenwillow Books, 1980.

Young children love the song. Having the book—although I wouldn't use it every time we sing the song—adds immensely to the fun.

Children love to act this out.

I trust the days of saying Santa brings gifts to good girls and boys are gone forever.

Good for fall.

Good repetition.

Glazer, Tom. *Do Your Ears Hang Low?* New York: Doubleday & Co., Inc., 1980.

———. *Eye Winker, Tom Tinker, Chin Chopper.* New York: Doubleday & Co., Inc., 1973.

———. *On Top of Spaghetti.* New York: Doubleday & Co., Inc., 1982.

Green, Norma B. *The Hole in the Dike.* New York: Harper & Row Publishers, Inc., 1975.

Hale, Irina. *Chocolate Mouse and Sugar Pig And How they Ran Away to Escape Being Eaten.* New York: Atheneum Publishers, 1979.

Hall, Donald. *Ox-Cart Man.* New York: The Viking Press, 1979.

Haywood, Carolyn. *A Christmas Fantasy.* New York: William Morrow and Co., 1972.

Hoban, Russell. *Bedtime for Frances.* New York: Harper & Row Publishers, Inc., 1976.

———. *A Birthday for Frances.* New York: Harper & Row Publishers, Inc., 1976.

———. *Bread and Jam for Frances.* New York: Harper & Row Publishers, Inc., 1964.

Hoberman, Mary Ann. *Yellow Butter Purple Jelly Red Jam Black Bread.* New York: The Viking Press, 1981.

Hogrogian, Nonny. *Apples.* New York: Macmillan Publishing Co., Inc., 1972.

———. *One Fine Day.* New York: Macmillan Publishing Co., Inc., 1974.

Hughes, Shirley. *David and Dog.* Englewood Cliffs, New Jersey: Prentice-Hall, Inc., 1981.

Hutchins, Pat. *Changes, Changes.* New York: Macmillan Publishing Co., Inc., 1973.

———. *Clocks and More Clocks.* New York: Macmillan Publishing Co., Inc., 1970.

———. *Don't Forget the Bacon.* New York: Greenwillow Books, 1976.

———. *Goodnight, Owl!* New York: Macmillan Publishing Co., Inc., 1972.   *Wonderful for acting.*

———. *Rosie's Walk.* New York: Macmillan Publishing Co., Inc., 1971.

———. *The Wind Blew.* New York: Macmillan Publishing Co., Inc., 1974.

Iela, Mari. *The Little Red Balloon.* New York: Barron's Educational Series, Inc., 1979.

Keats, Ezra Jack. *Jennie's Hat.* New York: Harper & Row Publishers, Inc., 1966.

———. *The Little Drummer Boy.* New York: Macmillan Publishing Co., Inc., 1972.

———. *Over in the Meadow.* New York: Four Winds Press, 1972.

———. *The Snowy Day.* New York: The Viking Press, 1962.

———. *Whistle for Willie.* New York: Penguin Books, 1977.

Kent, Jack. *The Fat Cat: A Danish Folktale.* New York: Scholastic Book Service, 1971.

Klika, Thom. *Rainbows.* New York: St. Martin's Press, 1979.

Krahn, Fernando. *How Santa Claus Had a Long and Difficult Journey Delivering His Presents.* New York: Delacorte Press, 1977.   *Good to act out.*

Kraus, Robert. *Herman the Helper*. New York: Windmill Books, 1974.

———. *How Spider Saved Halloween*. New York: Scholastic Book Service, 1980.

———. *Leo the Late Bloomer*. New York: Windmill Books, 1973.

———. *Milton the Early Riser*. New York: Windmill Books, 1972.

———. *Owliver*. New York: Windmill Books, 1974.

———. *Whose Mouse Are You?* New York: Macmillan Publishing Co., Inc., 1972.

Langstaff, John M. *Oh, A-Hunting We Will Go*. New York: Atheneum Publishers, 1974.

———. *Ol' Dan Tucker*. New York: Harcourt, Brace, Jovanovich, Inc., 1963.

Lear, Edward. *The Pelican Chorus and the Quangle Wangle's Hat*. New York: The Viking Press, 1981.

Lionni, Leo. *Alexander and the Wind-up Mouse*. New York: Pantheon Books, 1969.

———. *Alphabet Tree*. New York: Pantheon Books, 1968.

———. *The Biggest House in the World*. New York: Pantheon Books, 1968.

———. *A Color of His Own*. New York: Pantheon Books, 1976.

———. *Fish Is Fish*. New York: Pantheon Books, 1970.

———. *A Flea Story: I Want to Stay Here! I Want to Go There!* New York: Pantheon Books, 1977.

———. *Frederick*. New York: Pantheon Books, 1966.

The morals of these tales are extremely important for parents. Children at this age will enjoy the book, but won't get the point. Don't, for goodness' sake, push it!

The traditional song.

Some people think this is too advanced; I've found it works very well.

I have a windup mouse on hand to use. I could read this book ten thousand times and the children would still demand more!

A little advanced. I don't read this in circle, but to two or three children at a time.

We love snails and do this one during our annual Snail Week.

A chameleon story. Very good for the very young child.

The folk tale.

No words.

Too small to read to a large group.

No words.

On the small side for large group reading.

No words.

Act out for Pajama Day.

———. *Geraldine, the Music Mouse.* New York: Pantheon Books, 1979.

———. *The Greentail Mouse.* New York: Pantheon Books, 1973.

———. *Inch by Inch.* New York: Astor-Honor, 1962.

———. *In the Rabbitgarden.* New York: Pantheon Books, 1975.

———. *Little Blue and Little Yellow.* New York: Astor-Honor, 1959.

———. *Swimmy.* New York: Pantheon Books, 1963.

Littledale, Freya. *The Magic Fish.* New York: Scholastic Book Service, 1969.

Mayer, Mercer. *A Boy, a Dog and a Frog.* New York: The Dial Press, 1976.

———. *Ah-Choo.* New York: The Dial Press, 1976.

———. *Bubble, Bubble.* New York: Scholastic Book Service, 1980.

———. *The Great Cat Chase.* New York: Scholastic Book Service, 1975.

———. *Hiccup.* New York: The Dial Press, 1978.

———. *Just Me and My Dad.* New York: Golden Books, 1977.

———. *There's a Nightmare in My Closet.* New York: The Dial Press, 1968.

——— and Marianna Mayer. *A Boy, a Dog, a Frog and a Friend.* New York: The Dial Press, 1971.

McCloskey, Robert. *Blueberries for Sal.* New York: The Viking Press, 1948.

McDermott, Gerald. *Anansi the Spider. A Tale of the Ashanti.* New York: Holt, Rinehart & Winston, 1976.

McPhail, David M. *The Bear's Toothache.* Boston: Little, Brown and Co., Inc., 1972.

Miles, Miska. *Annie and the Old One*. Boston: Little, Brown and Co., Inc., 1971.

———. *Chicken Forgets*. Boston: Little, Brown and Co., Inc., 1976.

Murphy, Jill. *Peace at Last*. New York: The Dial Press, 1980.

Niland, Deborah. *ABC of Monsters*. New York: McGraw-Hill Book Co., 1978.

Nixon, Joan Lowery. *The Alligator Under the Bed*. New York: G. P. Putnam's Sons, 1974.

Orlick, Terry. *The Cooperative Sports and Game Book: Challenge Without Competition*. New York: Pantheon Books, 1978.

Pinkwater, Manus. The Big Orange Splot. New York: Hastings House Publishers, Inc., 1977.

Piper, Watty. *The Little Engine That Could*. New York: Platt & Munk Publishers, 1976.

Plath, Sylvia. *The Bed Book*. New York: Harper & Row Publishers, Inc., 1976.

Quackenbush, Robert. *Clementine*. New York: Harper & Row Publishers, Inc., 1976.

———. *She'll be Comin' round the Mountain*. New York: Harper & Row Publishers, Inc., 1973.

———. *Skip to My Lou*. New York: Harper & Row Publishers, Inc., 1975.

Sandburg, Carl. *The Wedding Procession of the Rag Doll and the Broom Handle and Who Was in It*. New York: Harcourt, Brace, Jovanovich, Inc., 1978.

A joy! One of the recent fruits of my compulsive looking for new materials. A delightful nighttime story, fun to act out. Needs no props. Ask the children where they go to find peace and quiet!

An absolutely necessary addition to your collection of books on games. The point here is that everybody wins and nobody loses! The author includes a special section on games for children three to seven years old and one for preschoolers as well.

A book for individualists.

Pajama Day.

Marvelous songs; the repetition here is a very desirable feature.

Seeger, Pete and Charles. *The Foolish Frog.* New York: Macmillan Publishing Co., Inc., 1973.

Segal, Joyce. *It's Time to Go to Bed.* New York: Doubleday and Co., Inc., 1979.   *Great for Pajama Day.*

Silverstein, Shel. *A Giraffe and a Half.* New York: Harper & Row Publishers, Inc., 1964.

————. *Where the Sidewalk Ends.* New York: Harper & Row Publishers, Inc., 1974.

Scott, Ann Herbert. *On Mother's Lap.* New York: McGraw-Hill Book Co., 1972.

Sendak, Maurice. *Chicken Soup with Rice.* New York: Harper & Row Publishers, Inc., 1962.

————. *Hector Protector.* New York: Harper & Row Publishers, Inc., 1965.

————. *In the Night Kitchen.* New York: Harper & Row Publishers, Inc., 1970.

————. *Nutshell Library: Pierre, One Was Johnny, Chicken Soup with Rice, Alligators All Around.* New York: Harper & Row Publishers, Inc., 1962.

————. *Where the Wild Things Are.* New York: Harper & Row Publishers, Inc., 1963.

Shulevitz, Uri. Dawn. New York: Farrar, Straus and Giroux, Inc., 1974.

Slobodkina, Esphyr. *Caps for Sale.* New York: Scholastic Book Service, 1976.   *A standard for acting.*

Spier, Peter. *Oh, Were They Ever Happy.* New York: Doubleday & Co., Inc., 1978.

————. *The Star Spangled Banner.* New York: Doubleday & Co., Inc., 1973.

Steig, William. *The Amazing Bone*. New York: Farrar, Straus and Giroux, Inc., 1976.

———. *Sylvester and the Magic Pebble*. New York: Windmill Books, 1969.

In French, Spanish, and English.

Stevens, Cat. *Teaser and the Firecat*. New York: Scholastic Book Service, 1977.

Stevenson, James. *That Terrible Halloween Night*. New York: Greenwillow Books, 1980.

Thaler, Mike. *How Far Will a Rubber Band Stretch*. New York: Four Winds Press, 1972.

Ungerer, Tomi. *Beast of Monsieur Racine*. New York: Farrar, Straus and Giroux, Inc., 1971.

Untermeyer, Louis, ed. *The Golden Treasury of Poetry*. New York: Western Publishers, 1959.

Vidal, Beatrice, illus. *Bringing the Rain to Kapiti Plain*. New York: The Dial Press, 1981.

Viorst, Judith. *Alexander and the Terrible, Horrible, No Good, Very Bad Day*. New York: Atheneum Publishers, 1972.

———. *Alexander, Who Used to Be Rich Last Sunday*. New York: Atheneum Publishers, 1978.

Good for acting. Lots of characters.

Westcott, Nadine. *I Know an Old Lady Who Swallowed a Fly*. Boston: Little, Brown & Co., Inc., 1980.

I don't read this; I just put it out.

Wildsmith, Brian. *Brian Wildsmith's ABC*. New York: Franklin Watts, 1973.

———. *The Circus*. New York: Oxford University Press, Inc., 1980.

———. *Fishes*. New York: Franklin Watts, 1968.

———. *Mother Goose*. New York: Franklin Watts, 1970.

Wood, Audrey. *Twenty-four Robbers*. New York: Child's Play International, Ltd., 1980.

Zemach, Harve. *Judge*. New York: Farrar, Straus and Giroux, Inc., 1969.

———. *Mommy, Buy Me a China Doll*. New York: Farrar, Straus and Giroux, Inc., 1975.

Zolotow, Charlotte. *Wake up and Goodnight*. New York: Harper & Row Publishers, Inc., 1971.

A chanting, jump-rope rhyme kind of book. It was our hands-down favorite at the Roseville Cooperative Preschool last year.

just for the record

I have already expressed my concerns about cassette and record players—that they can't hug, kiss, or make mistakes. But good recordings for young children can be a positive element in a child's life. The list I offer here is very brief; some of the records I recommend have movement songs in addition to quiet, soothing music. Many of the songs encourage child involvement, verbally and physically. The record list is only, of course, a start. Your children will have favorites not on this list, just as we all have favorites not on the Top Ten this week.

These records represent, however, a selection of the best available for the young child and for the preschool; I hope you will use them to set your standards for what is worth buying and using.

Ella Jenkins. *You'll Sing a Song and I'll Sing a Song. My Street Begins at My House. Looking Forward—Looking Back.* Folkways Records and Service Corporation, New York. Wonderful collection and treatment of traditional children's material and a great way to deal with the need to pass songs along from generation to generation; a must for everyone's library.

The Limelighters. *Through Children's Eyes*. Brass Dolphin Records (reissue). Recorded in 1961, this album is a collection of favorites. We especially enjoy "Morningtown Ride" for Pajama Day and "The Lollipop Tree" for Lollipop Day. The recording includes a wonderful version of "This Land is Your Land."

Steve Millang and Greg Scalsa. *We All Live Together*. Three vols. Youngheart Records, 1979. This is a contemporary collection of songs in a pop-rock musical style. Games and activities are explained in a "Leader's Guide" that encourages creativity and makes suggestions for expanding on activities and games.

Anne Murray. *Anne Murray Sings for the Sesame Street Generation*. Balmur Ltd., 1979. This is a good source for old favorites like "You Are My Sunshine," "Teddy Bears' Picnic," and "Inchworm."

Musical Adventures for Young Children, Reader's Digest Collection. A four-record collection of classical music geared to listening for the young child.

Hap Palmer. *The Feel of Music*. Educational Activities, Inc., Freeport, New York 11570. Hap Palmer. *Movin'*. Educational Activities, Inc., Freeport, New York 11570. The Hap Palmer records are child-centered activity recordings that encourage movement, basic skills in mathematics, recognition of color, and other basic skills. Our favorites are "Witches' Brew," "Movin'," "The Feel of Music," and "Getting to Know Myself." It's very important in using these records that the adults know the songs and that adults attempt to make the activities encouraged here absolutely and always *stress-free* for the child.

Raffi. *Singable Songs. More Singable Songs. The Corner Grocery Store. Baby Beluga. Rise and Shine*. Troubadour Records, Ltd. Available through Shoreline Records, Willowdale, Ontario. This upbeat Canadian singer spends most of his year touring and singing with young children, and it shows. Every song is sung in a key that all children can sing in and seems to have been chosen for the sheer joy of it.

Pete Seeger. *American Folk Songs for Children*. Folkways Records and Services Corporation, New York. The title says it all; another must for everyone's record library.

At home and at school, a good music library must contain a wide selection of classical music. I can't encourage you too strongly to experiment broadly in this area as well, in order to form children's tastes—not only for Western music, but for music of all cultures.

index